No Remorse

For Linus,
    Dot Moore
    9/19/11

John Wallace as a child. Right, in a familiar pose with pearl-handled pistol on his hip.

John Walton Wallace was a complex man! His personality and character, or lack of it, appeared to run to extremes. His laughing, jovial personality went with him to the electric chair. His uncontrolled anger, once described as "likened to an exploding tomato," caused his death sentence. His awareness of the law of corpus delicti prompted him to try to destroy the body of William Turner. His compassion brought him to the aid and care of the poor and the sick. He once asked, *"I wonder if*

Two women in his life: his wife, Josephine, left, and Dorothy Dunlap.

they will remember that I 'sat up' with that dead man long after his family had gone to bed?" He did nice things like that. His disappointment, frustrations and fears caused him to strike out at the innocent as well as the guilty, like William Turner, for whom he once had sympathy. He was heartless to the wife who loved him. To tell his story sixty years after his death is complicated, for most of the printed materials about him are in conflict, just like he was!

Wallace invested heavily in fine dairy cattle, which grazed in tranquil settings like this.

Now, dear reader, how can one write a historical book that tells of a crime which occurred six decades ago if using the printed materials? Interviews are just as problematic. Perhaps one should just go with the rumors and say that John Wallace was not electrocuted in the Tattnall Prison on November 3, 1950, but escaped to Texas, or was it Mexico? Was he a typical sociopath with no remorse, yet charming and helpful? Was he a real-life Dr. Jekyll and Mr. Hyde? Had he been damaged as a result of his father's death? Did he fail to have a normal upbringing by a mother who, he said, often told him, "Just do what you have to do, John,

Wallace's final resting place, the city cemetery in Chipley (now Pine Mountain), Georgia.

and don't let your conscience get in the way"? Did he receive an unfair trial with no chance of acquittal? Did he lie to the end or was he telling the truth as he knew it? This book is an attempt to get to know the *real* John Walton Wallace. A reading of "the real facts," as he often called them, may enlighten some, may cause further dispute among those who knew him or knew of him, or may only give "food for thought." But most assuredly, this book will bring forth the important question: Whatever happened to that handsome young fellow whose father proclaimed in a newspaper notice, "Hooray, it is a fine little boy!"

ALSO BY DOT MOORE

The Oracle of the Ages: Reflections on the Curious Life
of Fortune Teller Mayhayley Lancaster (with Katie Lamar; 2001)

NO REMORSE

The Rise and Fall of John Wallace

DOT MOORE

NewSouth Books
Montgomery | Louisville

NewSouth Books
105 S. Court Street
Montgomery, AL 36104

Library of Congress Cataloging-in-Publication Data

Moore, Dot, 1931–
No remorse : the rise and fall of John Wallace / Dot Moore.

p. cm.

Includes index.

ISBN-13: 978-1-58838-264-1 (trade cloth)
ISBN-10: 1-58838-264-8 (trade cloth)

1. Wallace, John, 1896–1950. 2. Murderers—Georgia—Biography.
3. Murder—Georgia—Case studies. I. Title.
HV6248.W197M66 2011
364.152'3092—dc23

2011027226

Design by Randall Williams

Printed in the United States of America by
Sheridan Books.

To the late
Miss Dorothy Dunlap,
A MUCH-MALIGNED WOMAN

Contents

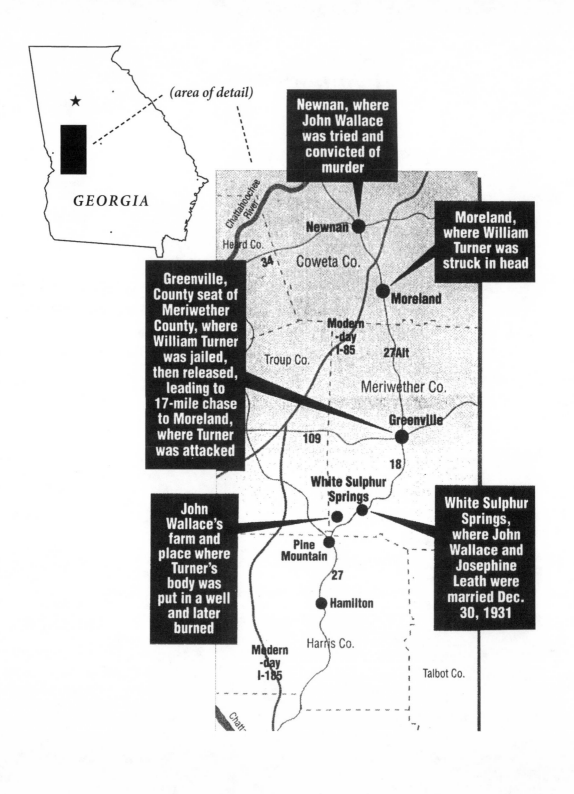

PREFACE

The Real Facts?

This book is about John Wallace, the Alabama-born Georgian who died in the electric chair in 1950. His crime was a sensation at the time and still rivets people sixty-plus years later. Three lengthy articles in nationally distributed magazines appeared around the time of the trial in 1948 and the subsequent appeals: *Master Detective*: "Case of the 41 Clues" by Allston C. Calhoun; *Real Detective*: "A Slayer's Fortune in Spades" by Jasper Haynes; and *True Detective*: "Prophecy of Doom" by C. C. Christopher. Later there was a full-length book, *Murder in Coweta County* by Margaret Anne Barnes, and there was a lengthy chapter in the book *Confessions of a Criminal Lawyer* written by Wallace's lead attorney, A. L. Henson. These books depict the trial differently.

In addition, more than fifty articles about the crime and trial were printed in the *LaGrange Daily News, Newnan Times, Atlanta Constitution, Atlanta Journal* and the *Columbus* (Georgia) *Ledger-Enquirer*. Vastly different. Mistakes abound.

Different reporters saw the case differently and got their information from persons who saw the details of the case differently. But the following facts are indisputable:

1. William (alias Wilson) Turner was killed by John Wallace.

2. The incident occurred April 20, 1948.

3. Turner was let out of the Meriwether County jail in Greenville, Georgia, around noon on the 20th.

4. Turner stopped at the Sunset Tourist Camp in the community of Moreland in Coweta County, Georgia.

5. John Wallace and Herring Sivell were seen apprehending Turner.

6. Wallace hit him in the head with the butt of a shotgun.

7. Two other men, Tom Strickland and Henry Mobley, were involved in some way with the altercation.

8. All four of these men were arrested and held in the Coweta County jail in Newnan, Georgia until June 14, 1948 when the five-day trial began.

9. Attorneys for the four men were A.L. Henson, Gus Huddleston, Kirk Whatley, Pierre Howard, Jack Allen and Fred New.

10. Attorneys for the State were Luther Wyatt and Meyer Goldberg.

11. The presiding judge was Sam Boykin.

AMONG THE CAST OF characters in this dramatic trial were the sheriffs of Coweta, Muscogee, and Meriwether counties. State enforcement officers and forensic personnel included J. C. Otwell, Pete Bedenbaugh, Jake Potts, Elzie Hancock, Jim Hillin, and Dr. Herman D. Jones. Fortune-teller Mayhayley Lancaster was among the witnesses. Reporters at the trial included Celestine Sibley and Hugh Park.

However, one will find it impossible to know the facts of the case from the printed materials. For instance:

1. Henry Mobley is named John Mobley, Tom Mobley, or Henry Mobley. He is a dairyman, a farmer or a worker in a Chipley garage or all of the above.

2. Tom Strickland is an uncle or a cousin.

3. Sheriff Potts learns of the altercation at Sunset Tourist Camp by owner Steve Smith calling him, by Julia Turner coming to see him in his office, or by a radio announcement.

4. Turner received a death blow at Sunset Tourist Camp, or was "whacked" on the head, or was pounded with a death blow across his scalp, or received a small cut on his ear, or was beaten by Sivell, or was beaten by Wallace; he fell on the ground, or fell into the back seat of a car, or was tossed into the front seat of the car which is sometimes black and blue and a Ford sedan or a pick-up truck.

5. Sivell was driving the car or John Wallace was driving the car.

6. A second car was also in the parking lot of Sunset, or the second car never arrived at Sunset, or there was no second car.

7. Turner had a brand new pick-up truck, or had a beat-up old pick-up truck which he paid cash for the week before or bought three years before or is making monthly payments.

8. Turner's murder was premeditated or was an accident.

9. John Wallace lived in a four-room house, or a six-room house, or a white-columned antebellum Greek Revival mansion.

10. Pete Bedenbaugh went down into the well searching for the body of William Turner, or J. C. Otwell went down into the well, or Elzie Hancock went down in the well, or was it Sheriff Lamar Potts who went down into the well?

11. Sheriff Lamar Potts went to see Mayhayley and got information, or J. C. Otwell and Jim Hillin went to see Mayhayley. Maybe they all went.

12. The information from Mayhayley was true; the information was false. Mayhayley's testimony about the visits was true or was a lie.

12. Turner was killed in Coweta County, or Turner was killed in Meriwether County.

No Remorse: The Rise and Fall of John Wallace will be classified as nonfiction, and it is. It also is a mystery story.

It is a tale of a child born into a family that was wealthy by the standards of the area and the time. John Wallace had prominent, well-connected parents, and a scholarly, pretty sister. The death of his father changed that. Why did the change of home and community position affect him and not his sister? Was this when he tended toward sociopathy? Or was he just an ordinary guy who often had temper tantrums?

Reaching adulthood, Wallace became enamored of the Dunlap family who lived across the road from his new Georgia home. Did he love the mother and/or the child? Did this more than thirty-year relationship draw him into begging to be buried with them?

The Spanish Flu debilitated Wallace. Did it make him impotent, sterile, and unable to make meaningful sexual relationships? Did his marriage, approaching the age of forty, mean anything to him? Why would he toss his wife's poetry, sewing (four homemade ties), and letters into the hands of Dorothy and Willie?

Wallace frequently treated his black workers with care and concern but then he also threatened and cajoled them, and he drowned, beat, and killed them when disobeyed. What manner of overseer was he? Or was his manner just the practice of the area to treat blacks with disdain?

Until the end of his life he denied killing William Turner in the manner charged and in the jurisdiction, Coweta County, which tried him for the murder. Two of his compatriots agreed with him until their dying days. To Wallace's end, he waited for his cousin Tom to come forth and tell the truth, for Tom was there, he said. Tom did not step forward. Why not?

(A recently-found note to Willie will allow the reader to solve one mystery.)

Wallace claimed that the courtroom witnesses lied. At least one did. Who else? Courtroom rules require defense counsel to be told about witnesses ahead of time, yet Wallace's lawyer had never seen nor heard of the most compelling witnesses against his client until they were brought into the courtroom. Why did Solicitor Wyatt, who claimed to be Wallace's friend, play so loose with the rules that are intended to ensure a fair trial? Did John Wallace ever have a chance?

Read on, gentle reader.

No Remorse

The courthouse in Chambers County, Alabama, where the births of cousins John Walton Wallace and Joe Louis (Barrow) occurred.

1

Going to Glass, Alabama

"I was born on a farm ten miles from old West Point, Georgia in Chambers County, Alabama" — **John Wallace, in trial testimony, June 20, 1948**

John Walton Wallace was born June 12, 1896, in Glass, Alabama, a small community that stretched along a narrow dirt road from a town called Fairfax all the way to the Riverview Cotton Mill which was perched high on the west bank of the Chattahoochee River. Many of the families in Glass were workers at the large mill. John Wallace's people were not, for they were landed gentry, holding more than eight hundred acres of farm land.

John Walton Wallace, named for his father's very respectable brother, was born in a two-story, high-roofed, unpainted frame house. It was the style out in the country *not* to paint the houses the shiny white typical of houses in the nearby towns, but to keep them dark. John's birthplace had been in the Wallace family since before 1840 when the first Walton Wallis (later changed to Wallace) family moved into Alabama from South Carolina. Walton and his wife, Nancy, had moved across Georgia in wagons and buggies, pulling their bare household goods, with twenty slaves following on foot. The caravan had stopped along the way for baby Mary to be born in Georgia.

Settling down in several houses, probably built of hewn logs cleared from their virgin forest, they had their own schoolteacher with them, for the Wallaces were always education-bent.

In time, the children who had made the journey, which included three children of Mrs. Wallace's widowed sister, married and settled in the formerly Creek Indian-occupied land. Their fortune grew as evidenced by their owning even more slaves as noted in the 1860 census. But the bottom fell out for the Walton Wallace family on January 11, 1861, when Alabama joined the Confederate States.

While there are no records of any of the Wallace men serving in the war—they were either too old or too young—the Wallaces suffered the same loss as their neighbors, particularly if they had slaves—the loss of free labor. By 1870, poor Mr. Walton Wallace was dead and buried in an unmarked grave in the Cusseta cemetery and his wife was destitute. She, too, died soon afterwards and is also buried in an unmarked grave. The land in the Glass community was all that was left to the once ambitious, successful family.

Their only Alabama-born son, Thomas, married a daughter of the Barrow family. They, too, had come into Chambers County around 1840, but from North Carolina, which generally spoke of a lesser aristocracy than South Carolinians. Members of neither family were considered Southern aristocrats, often defined as "a white family who lived in a big white house and never moved!" The Barrows had moved westward in wagons and buggies—sometimes called carriages—in hopes of finding economic success in the sparsely populated, uncultivated land in eastern Alabama.

The Barrow family found Alabama to be to their advantage. The first generation in Alabama, patriarch James Heath Barrow, acquired a plantation-type home, many sharecroppers, and was elected to the Alabama Legislature in 1872. Among his sharecropper families he also found a black woman who birthed a mulatto named Monroe, who birthed a half-Cherokee baby named Joe Louis Barrow who would gain international fame as simply Joe Louis, the "Brown Bomber," one of the greatest boxing champions of all time. He and our John Wallace were cousins across the race line.

Two other famous names lived nearby. All the school children knew of Pat Garrett, the hero who left Chambers County, moved out west and, as a western lawman, killed the infamous desperado, "Billy the Kid." There were books about Garrett.

But the most remarkable resident of Glass, Alabama, was John Howard Parnell, the brother of Charles Stuart Parnell, the "Uncrowned King of Ireland." From one of Ireland's greatest families, John Howard Parnell came to Glass to establish the Sunnyside Peach Farms. He lived in Glass for many years and his famous brother came to visit. John Howard Parnell eventually returned to Ireland to serve in the House of Commons until his death, or so the residents of Glass always said.

John Wallace's father, Welsey, would have known the famous Mr. Parnell.

John Walton Wallace, who was born to Thomas Jr. (called Welsey, his middle name), knew happiness in the large unpainted house located in the middle of an eight hundred-acre farm which was populated by his aunts and uncle, his grandparents, and cousins a-plenty. His mother and father had reportedly met while going to the West Point High School, a school which enjoyed an excellent reputation. The school also provided housing for those who lived further than a quick walk or ride to the school. One such boarding student was Myrtice Strickland, who lived in the White Sulphur Springs community in lower Meriwether County, Georgia.

When Myrtice was twenty-eight and Welsey was twenty-nine, they married in her home on what was then called Comer-Stovall Road, the ceremony being performed by neighbor and local preacher, S. D. Clements. The newlyweds moved into the Wallace house on the heavily traveled road in the center of Glass and soon joined the Hopewell Methodist Church.

IN ONE YEAR, THE Wallace's first child, Jean, was born. Two years later, on June 12th, John Walton was born. On June 17, 1896, in the *LaFayette Sun*, there was a notice, reading, *"Mr. Welsey Wallace is overjoyed. He said, 'Hooray, it is a fine little boy!'"*

Myrtice had plenty of help with her children. The Thomas family were tenants on the farm and lived right behind their house. The Thomases had a son that same summer and named him John Wallace Thomas. He would become the playmate for the handsome little boy, John, while his mother and father helped Myrtice around the house and farm.

It was a good time to be living in the lower eastern part of Chambers County. The mighty Chattahoochee River was only a few miles away, and it provided opportunities for fishing and for frolicking in the shallow waters in the summertime. The Riverview cotton mill provided jobs for white women and men who lived in the small "company houses" and paid rent to the company.

When John was six he joined older sister Jean in the local school, Bryson Academy.

He was ready to take on the world!

2

Going to School

*"I received my education at a small country school in that community." — **John Wallace, in trial testimony, June 20, 1948***

Bryson Academy was built in 1896, the same year John Wallace was born. White families who lived in Glass and could pay a small fee were encouraged to enroll their children in Bryson Academy. Once begun, the Academy building was quickly completed and had more than twenty pupils.

The Academy combined the names of William Jennings *Bry*an, who was then running his first campaign for the United States presidency, and Georgia Congressman Thomas E. Wat*son*, his running mate. The one-room school was in a big clapboard building with a tall prominent front door. In time, John was enrolled in the private school. Many years later alumni of the school stated that the school had excellent teachers who were knowledgeable in their subjects. Both Jean and John first developed their academic skills in the Bryson Academy.

While John was attending school his mother stayed at home maintaining the large house and even overseeing the feeding of day workers during the busier times of the farm year.

Father Welsey was different. Welsey had a great personality, excellent speaking skills, and was a leader of progressive thinking in his community. By the time John was born in 1896, Welsey was already busy around the community, often going to LaFayette, the county seat, to discuss election procedures and issues that were of interest to him. He was the Glass precinct captain and was thus responsible for honest elections in his district.

Welsey became deeply involved in the Southern Cotton Association (SCA), an organization made up of farmers of substance who believed that the price of cotton could be controlled by lessened production (a plan that was instituted during the Great Depression with economic success). Welsey was president of the group and its outspoken leader.

With the upcoming elections there appeared another notice in the *LaFayette Sun*: "We the undersigned Democratic voters of Beat 13 ask that our friends throughout the county assist in the election of T. W. Wallace to the office of county commissioner."

Welsey Wallace was elected to the Chambers County Board of Commissioners. He had received endorsements from his prominent neighbors, including Dr. C. R. Glass, for whom the community was named. His election was significant because the Board of Commissioners oversaw all the public interests of Chambers County. Apparently, with Welsey Wallace, there was little time left for the farm. It would soon be seen that he was living far beyond his means.

In early July 1907, when John Wallace was eleven, his father took seriously ill. It has been reported that Welsey had an attack of appendicitis.

He may also have been suffering from depression over his outstanding debts. In West Point he owed the J. J. Hagedorn store $692.10; Miller and Erwin $14.19; J. S. Horsley $65; Eady Baker Groceries $958.94; Hughely-McCulloh Company $354.10; and T. L. Varner $273.10. He owed a Dr. Hodges $62.35 and M. M. Hunt $7.41, both of Riverview; a Dr. Chambers of Langdale $13 and the R. V. Combs Company of Lineville $44.69. He was facing debts of more than $2,400 when he lay dying.

His death, on July 23, 1907, came in the middle of "lay-by" time when the Wallace crops were in the fields and there was little to do but watch cotton and corn grow. It was the practice of the farmers to borrow "seed money" to finance planting the crops and when harvest time came to repay the creditors. However, Welsey Wallace's bills were not all "seed money" but, rather money was also owed for groceries, a little amount to several doctors which may have been related to his impending death, and a large amount of money was owed for small and large items purchased on credit at the local department stores.

DEATH OF MR. T. W. WALLACE

After an illness of two weeks, Mr. T. Welsey Wallace, Junior, died at his home near Glass, Alabama, Wednesday afternoon, the 23rd instant.

He was one of Chambers County's most progressive farmers and was a public spirited, enterprising citizen. He was 40 years of age—just in the mid-day of an active and useful life.

His death comes as a blow not only to his devoted wife and to fond children but also to his community, county and state.

He was a member of the Methodist church. His remains are to be brought to West Point today, Wednesday, and funeral services are to be held at 4 P.M. by Reverend R. B. Morrow.

The interment will be at Pinewood Cemetery.

THE FUNERAL WAS HELD the following Wednesday and there was a large crowd: his large family, his many friends, and those who had worked with him in his political life. Despite the large amount owed, the Hagedorn Company furnished the casket, suitable clothes for burial, and the hearse—all for $91.25. The following March, Myrtice paid $50 in cash on the bill and the remainder was paid seven years later on April 15, 1915.

In August 1907, Alabama Governor Bibb Comer appointed Mr. R. T. Owens of Cusseta as county commissioner to fill the vacancy caused by the death of Welsey. "Mr. Owens is a prominent farmer and one of our best citizens," read the announcement.

Myrtice was named executrix of Welsey's estate. On September 4, the Chambers County Probate Judge placed a pro forma announcement in the local newspapers: "If you have claims against the estate, file it." When the judge was presented with Welsey's bills, against only $325 in liquid assets, an inventory of his part of the farm was ordered and entered into the court in October. The inventory revealed farm equipment and several farm animals.

Myrtice was unable to pay the bills. The county sheriff was then appointed to administer the Wallace estate, and C. S. Moore, a local attorney, was appointed guardian ad litem for both John and Jean. Later, when Moore's term as guardian expired, Charles E. Fuller was appointed guardian for the two children. The debts, the inventory, and the assets were published in the newspapers and posted on the walls of the courthouse and in other public buildings throughout Chambers County and may have been advertised in the surrounding counties in Alabama and Georgia, as well.

On April 11, 1910, Welsey's brother, John Wallace, was able to subdivide the large farm and put it up for auction. The funds from the sale allowed Myrtice some financial relief but not enough to retire all the outstanding debts. She later expressed anger when she learned that her brother-in-law had been the highest bidder and so retained the farm. It was during this time that her father, Zeke Strickland, stepped forward and helped his older daughter financially.

THE SHAME OF IT all. The embarrassment of it all. From growing up in a prominent Alabama family and attending a good private school, the going-on-fourteen-year-old boy, John Walton Wallace, his sister, Jean, and mother Myrtice were reduced to living with others. For unknown reasons, the prominent LaFayette Lanier family, with their two children and six live-in servants, received the little Wallace family on their premises. The Wallaces were living with the Laniers when the 1910 census was taken on May 9th.

After the death of his father, John's personality changed from sweet and obedient to that of an aggressive, pugnacious boy. He was large for his age and used his height and weight to bully his classmates. He fought both boys and girls. One classmate, Nim Williams, was often the object of his abuse. Daily, John pushed and shoved him until the boy's mother, Mrs. Charlie Williams, went to see Myrtice and pled with her to stop the torment. The following day, John was even more vicious. Nim then gathered stones and pelted John on his way home from school. After that, Nim was left alone and soon the boys became friends.

The estate of Welsey Wallace was finally settled December 9, 1911, thanks to Myrtice's father. The family was now free to leave Chambers County, Alabama. The problems at Bryson Academy may have abated by then, but John's behavior had now become a problem in the community. Myrtice was approached by a law enforcement officer who advised her to get John out of Chambers County before he got into some real trouble.

Myrtice agreed. In the summer of 1912, she, Jean, and John moved back to her family home in Georgia. Jean went on to a successful career in education in the Atlanta area, but Myrtice and John called Meriwether County, Georgia, home for the rest of their lives.

Bryson Academy students, 1900, before John was old enough to attend.

Bryson Academy students, 1904. John is believed to be in this photo.

Left, Ezekiel LaFayette "Zeke" Strickland.
Below, the Strickland home.

The young John Walton Wallace grew up in the Hopewell Methodist Church at Glass, Alabama.

HOPEWELL
METHODIST CHURCH

The origins of Hopewell M.E. Church date to religious meetings held by Rev. James M. Spear soon after his coming to Chambers County in 1839. An 1841 Class Paper names 48 white and 6 black members. The oldest written record entitled "Hopewell M.E. Church" is dated April 1843. It lists 44 members and names trustees James M. Spear, Hardy Hancock, Robert B. Everitt, Osborne Robinson and Micajah Wardlaw. A house of worship erected near the Spear home was destroyed in a storm shortly after Rev. Spear's death in November 1852. Both he and his wife, Margaret Everitt Spear are buried at this first location.

ERECTED BY THE HISTORIC CHATTAHOOCHEE COMMISSION
AND HOPEWELL UNITED METHODIST CHURCH
150TH ANNIVERSARY
1989

Today, much of rural and small-town Alabama and Georgia where Wallace was raised and lived has been abandoned.

3

Going to Meriwether County, Georgia

"I went to Gordon Military Institute at Barnesville, which was a military academy. I later went to Young Harris College, left there in 1914. In 1918 I went to the Army. I have an Honorable Discharge from the Army" — **John Wallace, in trial testimony**

When Myrtice arrived in her family home with teenagers Jean and John in tow, she was returning to the house where she had been born, grown up, and married. Her parents, Nancy Jo Davis and Ezekiel LaFayette Strickland Sr., called "Zeke," had built the large commodious house when they married in February of 1865 just when the Civil War was winding down. Her brother, Mozart, who never married, still lived with his parents. It was then and there that John really got to know his Uncle Mozart, who became a father-figure to him for the rest of his life.

Of Myrtice's family, brother Mondant was long dead of natural causes; brother Eli, also unmarried, lived down the road; and brother Henry Maynard was married to one of the nearby Hasty girls and lived farther south, nearer Chipley. Brother John Mercer was also married to one of the Hasty girls and they lived down Stovall Road.

Sister Inez had married and moved away only to be heard of again when she returned to the family as a corpse to be buried in the Davis-Strickland cemetery.

Myrtice was home; her children were not. Jean was already pursuing her education away from the family for she dreamed of becoming a teacher. John was soon enrolled at the Gordon Military Academy for a tortuous year of military-type drills, strict discipline, and endless classroom lessons. School records show that he attended Gordon for the academic year 1913–14.

The following year John Wallace was a student at Young Harris College, a two-year Methodist college in north Georgia, two hundred miles away. There he continued to develop his writing skills and was a studious, charming, and popular student. Throughout his life, he treasured his days there, and his classmates were diligent in keeping in touch with him. Many years later, in a letter to Governor Herman Talmadge, Wallace's sister Jean told of his sending three or four students to Young Harris College at his expense. Several of his former Young Harris classmates visited him on death row.

After his experience at Young Harris College (he did not graduate), John Wallace returned to the White Sulphur Springs community and lived in a newer house down the road from his grandparents. He may have just then begun to learn the trade of making corn whiskey; the country was in the throes of Prohibition and distilleries were beginning to close all over the United States. Any amount of any kind of alcohol was at a premium and could be sold at a great price.

When war broke out in Europe in 1914, the little John Wallace family was still enjoying the good times of the country's economy, although the Stricklands and their neighbors were now selling cotton for as little as fourteen cents a pound, when it had once sold for forty cents a pound.

In 1915, the Mexican boll weevil arrived in Meriwether County. It is no wonder that the lush soil "out West" appealed to Southerners like Myrtice Strickland Wallace. She had first bought land in Texas in 1911!

Neighbors Miss Willie Webb and Joe Hill Dunlap had married in 1914. They were the parents of a son, Joe Hill Dunlap Jr., born March 19, 1915. John Wallace and younger Dunlap would later lie near each other in the Chipley cemetery.

In 1916, the Wallace and Strickland families experienced a terrible shock when Myrtice's brother Eli was killed by gunshot in the front yard of the Strickland home. Brother John Mercer Strickland had killed him. It was said that they were arguing over a woman. No charges were entered against John Mercer, and Eli was quietly buried in the family cemetery. Such a death in this part of the rural South rarely called for an investigation by law officials.

The entry of the United States into the First World War affected many of the young men in Meriwether County. John Wallace was among the four million Americans who were drafted. John received written notice to report to the Draft Board of Meriwether County in Greenville on September 4, 1918. Military records show that he stated that he was born in Glass, Alabama, on June 12, 1896, was twenty-two years old, was tall, had brown hair and blue eyes.

John was probably sad to leave a baby he loved so much: Dorothy Dunlap had been born February 6, 1918, and she often said that she was born in the old Strickland home place. She was only a little more than four months old when John got word that he was being drafted. We will learn more about their relationship later.

After his draft board interview in Greenville, John Wallace was assigned to the campus of Alabama Polytechnic Institute, now Auburn University. He was to report on October 1. There, a newly improvised program, which was to be one of the largest military training units in the South, the Student Army Training Corps (S.A.T.C), was being developed. On October 1st, he was escorted to the S.A.T.C. office, assigned housing, given an Army uniform, and designated a private. He was told that even though there were nearly one thousand other soldiers on the campus, he had been selected to be among the three hundred who could participate in a program of vocational education. He could choose among a great variety of trades: auto mechanics, pipe fitting, sheet metal work, welding, carpentry, blacksmithing, and twenty other trades. It is not recorded which course he chose, only that he began to attend classes.

Seemingly unknown to this military establishment, a severe form of influenza, the Spanish Flu, had already broken out in January 1918 and was sweeping across the world. It appeared in Florence, Alabama, in late July. Strangely, small children and older adults were spared, but healthy young adults were not immune to "the grippe," as it was often called in Georgia.

Where young adults were quartered, as in military units, the influenza first took a mild form, but by the late summer of 1918, up to a third of the influenza sufferers were reporting increasingly hard symptoms which included bronchial pneumonia. Because the virus seemed to spread more quickly in cold weather when people confined themselves with others indoors, the southern part of the United States was generally spared in the midst of a very, very hot summer. But by fall, the virus had reached the South. Big time.

Within the first week of the training program, many of the students began to have chills and fever. Unable to handle the influenza pandemic, the S.A.T.C. leadership began arranging to close the program. They announced that those who appeared to be the sickest were to be transferred to the infirmary. Typical of those who had heard that "folks are dying in the infirmary," E. T. Daniel, one of John's fellow soldiers, was able to get a train ticket to his home in LaGrange. When he arrived at the train station he was unable to walk, and fellow passengers had to carry him off the train. In time, Daniel did recover.

Many of the S.A.T.C. students were transferred to other military bases around the country after the program was completely closed down by October 20th. John Wallace was not so fortunate. He was very sick.

Wallace was quickly moved to the Fort Meade Hospital in Baltimore, Maryland, a hospital which had gained a reputation for caring for those who were victims of all kinds of epidemics. It was said that he had been there for several months before his mother learned of his whereabouts.

He languished in the Maryland hospital until he was discharged from the Army on June 4, 1919. The pandemic diminished in the winter of 1919 but not before fifty million people worldwide had died, including seven hundred thousand in the United States and nearly eight thousand in Georgia.

John Wallace had been in the army eight months and three days. He got an honorable discharge, as he often bragged. Many years later, a close family friend said, "His bout with the Spanish Flu messed up his brain while he was overseas." He never went overseas, so there must be other reasons to explain his erratic behavior afterwards. Had the flu ruined his mind? Perhaps even made him impotent? Perhaps altered his personality? Current research does not say.

However, later research has indicated that those who were exposed to this particular virus would become immune to all future viruses and enjoy good health for the rest of their normal lives.

Electrocution, however, is not normal.

John Wallace as a WW I era soldier.

4

Going to Texas

"Well, Otis, I don't think we are going to make that trip to Texas this summer." — **John Wallace to Otis Cornett, November 3, 1950**

When John Wallace returned from the Maryland hospital, he got back into the swing of things—that is, making corn liquor. He still lived in the small house down the road from his grandparents' home, and his mother was living with him, perhaps even providing resources for him. Perhaps she may have worried that he was not yet well enough to live alone.

He was busy making friends and spent lots of time across the road with his favorite family, the Dunlaps. Baby Dorothy was only two years old and was his favorite person, even then. He sometimes worked in the fields and in his mother's garden. Not often.

Myrtice had found the Rio Grande Valley of lower Texas in 1911 when she still lived in Alabama. John sometimes went there with her to visit and tried his hand at raising fruit and vegetables. Several of their White Sulphur Springs neighbors had also discovered the Rio Grande Valley. Exaggerated rumors, and some true stories, of the area were coming back to the Georgians, and like the gold rush of California in 1849, many of the eager and resourceful farmers were quickly drawn to Texas. Another reason: the area was isolated, and those who were fearful of arrests and trials for bootlegging and other crimes could find security and safety in the Rio Grande Valley.

The Rio Grande Valley is a delta that is fed by the seasonally robust Rio Grande River, the same as in Egypt with the mighty Nile River. During the year when the rains were heavy, the river flooded the dry, sandy soil and spread rich dirt from upstream, making a perfect soil for growing vegetables and fruit, especially citrus. However, heavy rains sometimes washed the soil away and then the area suffered with poor soil that was of little value for farming until agricultural specialists took hold.

The land had been desolate for eons until an extensive program of irrigation, on a very large scale, was developed at the turn of the twentieth century. Then in 1904 the first of several railroad lines came into the area, making the shipping of fruit and vegetables more viable and profitable. The trains carried settlers into the Rio Grande Valley, too.

By 1921, Cameron County, one of the four counties of the Rio Grande Valley (the others were Hidalgo, Willis, and Starr), was renowned for its subtropical climate, fertile soil, and sunny weather—all excellent conditions for growing fruit and vegetables. There was also grassy land for cattle to feed upon and, across the border, there was cheap labor. Myrtice chose the town of La Feria (Spanish for "the fair"), a small town of only two square miles, which had a population of only two hundred English-speaking residents—Spanish-speaking Mexicans were not counted; they were not citizens.

Myrtice bought some land in La Feria, again with help from her father. She did not plan to establish residency, like their former neighbors the Brookses, but to raise produce which she could sell. Their own land in Meriwether County, Georgia, had become packed, and the nutrients and fertilizer were being washed away from the hard dirt by pounding spring and summer rains. Even a vegetable garden required constant digging and weeding on Strickland Road, while in La Feria the soil quickly provided lush vegetables and fruit. The pink grapefruit, only grown in the Rio Grande

Valley, was becoming popular all over the United States. Those who owned the trees where the grapefruit grew in high clusters, looking for all the world like hanging grapes (hence the name), were becoming well-off farmers. John and his mother were always interested in making money.

Also of interest to John Wallace and his visitors, and maybe to his mother, was a variety of birds in La Feria which were not common back in Meriwether County. Later, when incarcerated in a Georgia jail, he wrote, "If I could just see the birds just one more time, I would be happy." When he was in La Feria at the right time, he also marveled at the Monarch butterflies on their annual flight back and forth to Mexico. John Wallace was a nature lover.

When John went to Texas he usually carried a friend with him, such as Otis Cornett. When Myrtice went to Texas without her son, she was accompanied by a peg-legged black worker. Together they would gather the produce, sell some, then whatever they could not sell, they would pack into the truck and bring back to Meriwether County. At home, she would sometimes share her largess with her neighbors. She always used the vegetables for canning.

One of John's former neighbors, Comer Brooks, worked land for the Wallaces while also working his own. As usual, John Wallace's friendly manner brought new friends to his Texas lodging, and one family, the Hammetts, originally from LaGrange, Georgia, became life-long friends.

Once he discovered that one of the Hammet daughters was seriously ill and required special treatments which were not available in isolated Cameron County. He brought her back to his home in Georgia to get her well. Later, he sent her to his alma mater, Young Harris College. She was indebted to him and later said in a public hearing, "He is like a father to me."

In the Rio Grande Valley, John Wallace had found his own vacation site, a place to take his friends, and a place to get away from home. It was also an opportunity to make extra money while working alongside his mother, whom he adored.

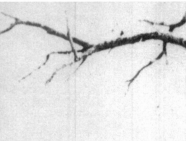

Top and right, Wallace and
some of his Texas friends.
Above, a Mexican guide's card
that Wallace kept.

5

Going to Jail and the Altar

"In 1918, I became involved in the liquor traffic. In September '28 I was sentenced. I got home in the early thirties." — **John Wallace**

In 1921 John Wallace bought 184 acres of land from his neighbors, the Hastys, and 127.5 acres from his Uncle Mozart. In 1925, he picked up a lien on a small farm of just eight acres. Then, though it turned out to be a poor investment, he bought eight lots in the development town of Stovall which was just down the road from his home. On December 2, 1925, he bought 199.4 acres from his neighbor A. E. Tigner. There was more. In the next twenty-five years, he would own nearly thirty pieces of property, some large, some small.

The extra money from his mother's La Feria lands was not as forthcoming as they had hoped. To pay for his ever-increasing land purchases, Wallace found it necessary to increase production in his whiskey-making.

When Prohibition came into its full power on January 17, 1920, and the legitimate national distilleries were closed, the "Strickland Distilleries" were poised to supply alcohol in a big way. John Wallace's stills, like those of his Uncle John Mercer, were huge, the size of a train car! They were operated day and night by black men who lived on his land and were overseen by him and his Uncle Mozart. Tales of the train stops and the whiskey being loaded onto train cars destined for Chicago spread throughout Meriwether and Harris counties. The large production of corn liquor was even talked about in LaGrange, the Troup County seat. It is not surprising that "revenuers," agents from the Alcohol Tax Unit of the Revenue Department, would soon move against the Wallace-Strickland enterprise.

John Wallace was "busted" on September 26, 1926, and again on March 3, 1928. He and his Uncle Mozart were tried for both arrests in the federal courts in Columbus. They were convicted and sentenced to two years in the federal prison in Atlanta— the Fulton Tower, as it was better known. John and his uncle were allowed to share a cell; they were roommates.

While they were in prison, Myrtice ignored the absence of her son and her brother.

Daughter Jean had become a well-known educator, had married James Willis Mozley when she was twenty-five and now had a son, a "junior," who was called Willis. They Mozleys often drove from Decatur, just outside of Atlanta, to visit Jean's family in White Sulphur Springs.

During one visit, little Willis noticed John's absence. "Grandma, where is Uncle John?" he asked.

Without a flinch, Myrtice answered, "He is in Atlanta. On business." That reply seemed to satisfy the little boy. John had been in the prison for a year at that time.

John and Uncle Mozart got out of prison before serving their full two years. Later Myrtice said they were sent home because of "good behavior." While that was probably true, a note attached to his records states that John "turned in a couple of moonshiners to the revenuers and to the judge," which may have hastened his release. The prison records also state that John was "good-natured, jovial, and fat."

When he returned home from the Tower, John Wallace turned more to social affairs in the community. While Myrtice was often seen at the summer Chautauqua at Warm Springs where there were lectures, music, and nightly moving pictures, John was spending time in nearby Chipley, in Harris County, where he now owned a warehouse building on the main street. He was often seen in the bank visiting his friend, Roy Askew, a cashier who later rose to bank president. Wallace was in and out of the stores on the main street of Chipley. He was friendly to everyone, greeting people with a big smile and a high-raised hand. However, he had already gained a reputation as a hot-tempered man who harshly ruled the blacks who lived and worked on his farm.

One day while walking with his friend Henry Mobley in Chipley, John was told that crossing the street in front of them was a black man who was defaulting on a loan. Henry had only recently taken a part-time job as a collector for Major Kimbrough, operator of a successful horse and mule business in Chipley.

When there was a pause in the black man's walk, John Wallace swiftly moved closer to him and yelled, "Why don't you pay up, nigger?" The black man turned around at the loud voice, looked at the two men and said nothing. He seemed to be staring at John Wallace and Henry Mobley.

A loud "blam" was heard. John Wallace had shot him. As the poor man was writhing and dying on the ground, John Wallace walked up to him, took a knife out of his own pocket, and placed it in the hand of the dying man. Then he shouted out to all who could hear, "Self-defense. Self-defense." That was the end of that. While recent literature attests to his complete control of law enforcement in Meriwether County, this incident happened in Harris County. In those days of complete Jim Crow segregation, the death of a black person did not always result in a prosecution or even an investigation. Eight decades later, Chipley residents can still show a visitor the spot where the poor man was killed by John Wallace.

John often went to the beautiful Meriwether White Sulphur Springs Hotel to have lunch and/or dinner and to visit with his Uncle Henry Maynard Strickland and his wife Ida Belle (Hasty). That he had just been released from prison caused no ostracism. Not only was it unimportant because he was the powerful John Wallace, but at that place and in that time, incarceration for bootlegging was a common event and was socially acceptable. John Wallace was among close friends and understanding relatives.

It was at the Springs Hotel that he met Josephine Leath. She was almost eighteen, he was thirty-five.

Josephine had visited the area all of her young life. Her grandmother was a Hasty; her father, John William Leath, had grown up in Chipley and moved to Blountstown, Florida, when he was a young man. There, he had risen to prominence, married "Josie" Rhoden in 1906 (a transplant from Berrien County, Georgia), became an officer during World War I, and had been elected a circuit judge more than five times when Josephine met John Wallace.

Josephine was unusually beautiful, with a slim figure, long brown hair, and smiling eyes. However, it was said that she was not well and had left her senior high school class in Blountstown to come to stay with her aunt, "Miss Ida Belle," until she could return to school. She never did.

She caught the eye of John Wallace. She was probably the prettiest woman he had ever seen. She was also "family," since his uncle (Henry Maynard) was married to her aunt (Ida Belle). Within six months, the wedding of John Wallace and Josephine Leath had been arranged. His mother, Myrtice, was not happy.

Early on Wednesday, December 30, 1931, John Wallace went to the courthouse in Greenville and got a marriage license, which was recorded in Marriage Book I, page 533, in the office of the Meriwether County Probate Judge.

The *Meriwether Vindicator* printed the details of the wedding.

LEATH-WALLACE

A beautiful wedding was that of Miss Josephine Leath to Mr. John Wallace which took place Wednesday afternoon, December 30 at 5:30 at Meriwether White Sulphur Springs Hotel.

The hall room and lobby were beautifully decorated for the occasion in smilax, ferns and cut flowers. An aisle was formed from the staircase to an improvised altar by garlands of smilax interspersed with white pedestals which burned white tapers. A quantity of these tapers also burned on the altar, piano and mantels.

Before the ceremony, Miss Sybil Strickland played "Until" and "O, Promise Me" on the violin accompanied by Mrs. P. L. Hopkins. To the strain of the Lohengrin Wedding March, the Reverend J. J. Davis of Atlanta, entered and took his place before the altar. Next came the groom and his best man, Mr. Pope Davis of Chipley.

Miss Cecile Strickland, a cousin of the bride, was maid of honor and was beautifully gowned in blue and carried a bouquet of pink roses and snapdragons.

The bride entered with her brother, Richard L. Leath of Florida by whom she was given away. She also was beautifully gowned in blue with tan hat, shoes and gloves and carried a beautiful bouquet of pink roses and valley lilies.

After the ceremony, the guests were invited into the dining room where sandwiches, punch, salted nuts and mints were served.

The young couple left during the evening for a short trip after which they will be at home to their friends at their handsome country home near the Springs.

Mrs. Ada DeLoach, reporter

It is also said that there was no trip, only a few days and nights spent in one of the cottages on the grounds of the Springs Hotel, the nicest place in that part of Georgia. More than one hundred rooms were inside the main building and there were several charming cottages clustered around the hot springs (the same springs later frequented by President Franklin D. Roosevelt). The bubbling fountains were surrounded by flower gardens. The hotel even had tennis courts, a bowling alley, and a swimming pool. It was as lush as a European spa and resort. It was a perfect place for a wedding and a honeymoon.

Soon the married couple was living in his small house on the Strickland Road. There were two bedrooms, a kitchen, a sitting room, a front and a back porch which overlooked the lake which he had recently built. But it was far from "handsome." John Wallace had never been pretentious; he never had a fine car, only the old Ford A-Model roadster which had been a family car for many years. There were no fine clothes, not even a telephone!

Josephine joined the Chipley Methodist Church on January 28, 1932, a month after the wedding. She was "sprinkled," for it was written in the church records that she had a "conversion." The Chipley Methodist Church was the Leaths' church and a plaque on the wall attested to her great-grandfather's charter membership. Interestingly, the Reverend James Allen, the father of the minister who would officiate at John Wallace's funeral, was the minister when Josephine joined the church, but he had not performed the wedding ceremony. Rather, Reverend Davis, a former minister, came from Atlanta. John did not join the church with Josephine then or at any other time. Ever.

Perhaps because her parents were in the middle of a divorce, they had not come to the wedding; instead, her older brother gave her away. John's mother did not attend the wonderful wedding, either. Perhaps she was upset with "her" John getting married, maybe she did not approve of their age differences, or maybe, for some unknown reason, she just didn't like Josephine.

A little more than one month after the wedding, February 4, 1932, Myrtice called in a local attorney, and with three of her neighbors as witnesses, she wrote her will. She left everything to her daughter, Jean. Everything.

The marriage of John Wallace and Josephine Leath was not getting off to a good start.

6

Going to the Whiskey Stills

*"The economic situation was very adverse at that time. Practically everyone was broke. I had lost about what holdings I had. I struggled along for five years. In 1935, I again fell from grace." — **John Wallace testimony, June 20, 1948***

By 1932, the agents of the Revenue Department were again onto the whiskey-makers. Elzie J. Hancock, the leading agent from the Columbus office, hung around White Sulphur Springs and other sparsely populated areas in his district. He was good at what he did. Unlike others who worked within the agency, Elzie, (often called "E. J.") said, "I always worked in the field. But then back then we had more moonshiners . . . and they didn't mind shooting and they didn't mind who they shot."

The most notorious of these was John Strickland, whose half-moon corner of Meriwether County, belonging to him and his family, was openly and arrogantly called 'The Kingdom.'

Strickland using a 100-horsepower engine and vats that were twelve feet wide, ran three shifts around the clock. He was supplied with sugar shipped in by train from New Orleans and had it delivered to a store front on the railroad siding. The liquor was then shipped out in milk cans by railcar with a false siding; the bill of lading marked 'lumber.'

The hirelings who worked for the Stricklands were easy to run down and catch, but it was Strickland himself that the Prohibition agents wanted to apprehend.

Colorful, clever, and ruthless, John Strickland costumed himself in balloon-sleeved white shirts, a black vest, and a pair of pearl–handled pistols which he never took off. Those who knew him well said he not only wore them in the house, but even when he went to bed, in case he should be accosted in the night.

No one dared cross John Strickland and if they did, they didn't live to tell about it. Strickland's temper was so quick and he draws so fast that no one was sure of the toll they had taken.

In the swamp one night in October (19) 1932, I and several other Prohibition Agents lay in wait at the liquor still pit waiting for Strickland to arrive and check the mash. When he did, I rose up out of the brush and said,

"Halt. We're federal officers."

John Strickland's response was a rain of bullets.

"I returned the fire, and John Strickland fell dead in the still yard.

John Mercer Strickland was quietly buried in the Davis-Strickland cemetery. His death certificate simply says that he died of a "gunshot."

His wife, Minnie Hasty, had left long before the killing. It was his daughter, Cecile, who had been the maid of honor at the Leath-Wallace wedding only ten months before.

Afterwards there was a big sale at John Strickland's house, and many people pored over his possessions. One former neighbor, then living in La Feria, Texas, wrote wondering if daughter Cecile got any insurance money. John Wallace may have gotten the pearl-handled pistols because he was later photographed wearing a pearl-handled pistol. He also gave a pearl-handled pistol to his neighbors, the Dunlaps, for their safety.

It is clear that hotheadedness and shooting and indifference to killing ran in the Srickland-Wallace temperament. Elzie J. Hancock told writer Margaret Anne Barnes that, "John Wallace, nephew of the notorious John Strickland, had inherited the clan's leadership from his uncle and his lawless ways, figuring that if a man needed killing, that was reason enough."

In addition to the senseless killing of the black man on the street of Chipley, Wallace also killed one of his black workers in an unprovoked dispute on the dirt road in front of his house. He had threatened killing others who were walking down the road at the time.

Even though national Prohibition ended in December 1933, Georgia, like most Southern states, continued to prohibit the making or transport of whiskey. There was still a demand for corn liquor.

The killing of John Mercer Strickland by Elzie Hancock apparently taught John Wallace nothing. He was again arrested by one of the agents of the Revenue Department; his neighbor Joe Dunlap was arrested, too. They were tried in Columbus in the courtroom of Judge Bascom Deaver, a federal judge who had been appointed by President Grover Cleveland. Wallace was given a sentence of three years as this was his second conviction (it was Joe's first).

In the sentencing John Wallace was granted a reprieve, of sorts. First, he was given six months to get his farm in good order. At the end of those six months, John Wallace again appealed to Judge Deaver for a six-month extension, which the judge granted.

When John Wallace finally appeared in Judge Deaver's office to begin his sentence, he assured the judge that he only wanted to return to his farm, be a faithful family man, and a good citizen who no longer had any desire to make liquor. On the basis of this, the judge reduced his three-year sentence to nine months. Apparently, John Wallace had charmed the esteemed judge, who was said to be a friend of President Franklin Roosevelt. John Wallace always said that he had been given a presidential pardon, one of the more than three thousand pardons Roosevelt granted—more than any other president of the United States has ever given!

While he and neighbor Joe Dunlap were away, Joe's wife, Willie, sent the following poem to John Wallace:

REMINISCING OF THE DAYS, PAST AND PRESENT

Yesterday I loved you—
Loved you far too much,
But today, I shrink away
From your slightest touch.
Yesterday my love for you was true—
But today, I fake it,
Don't complain—you had your chance
And you didn't take it.

Willie wrote the poem while "sitting in my room, watching the hogs roam and seeing Josephine and Pope playing dominoes." John Wallace kept Willie's poem and later gave it to Dorothy. Was Dorothy in fact a product of that love?

WHEN JOHN WALLACE RETURNED home from prison this time he indeed had made a change in his life: he was no longer a farmer, but a dairy man. In prison, apparently, he had learned of the scientific production of milk when the milk cows were bred properly. He immediately began to invest in Guernsey milk cows.

His Guernseys were easily recognized by their fawn/light brown color with large white spots. They slowly moved across his pastures eating grass six times a day and chewing their cud for eight hours. They were gentle, easy to breed and to give birth, and his cows gave more golden milk than had been seen locally before. The Guernsey milk was also easily made into cheese, butter, and ice cream. Unfortunately, these cows were very expensive. John Wallace later testified that he had given more than $3,000 for just one of his many cows.

His dairy farm was eminently successful. He sold milk in Columbus, Greenville,

Chipley, and LaGrange. When in LaGrange one day, he learned that there was a very good market for the milk and milk products. He rented a building on Greenville Street, right off the Square.

A former worker, Howard Kenney, from Montgomery, told this story many years after working for John Wallace in LaGrange:

"One day in 1938 John Wallace came to my daddy and asked for some help in developing a pasteurizing system for his dairy milk. Our family was already doing that. A state law had been passed that said if you sold milk to the public it had to be pasteurized. Safe to drink. My daddy told him that I knew how to do that and he would let me go and work for him. Mr. Wallace told him that he had already rented a store building. He said his brother-in law (I learned that it was Mrs. Wallace's brother, Richard L. Leath) had already ordered and installed the pasteurization equipment.

"The first day I went there to work, I saw a large sign on the outside of the building that said, SUPERIOR DAIRY. At opening time, Mr. Wallace drove up in a black, pick-up truck, loaded with ten-gallon milk cans. He was a big, heavy-set man and completely bald-headed. He was strong. He lifted those big cans by himself and brought them into the shop. All this time, there was a pretty young woman sitting up front in the pick-up, staring straight ahead. She took her time getting out of the pick-up and came on inside. She walked straight past me, not speaking, but had a sorta' sweet smile on her face. She went straight to a desk in the back of the store. I watched as she sat down and started fooling with some papers.

"In the meantime two of the other men who were working there, the brother-in-law and another man, named Cecil Perkerson, were helping with the milk cans. I remember that Mr. Wallace shouted out to me, 'Fresh from the udder,' which I thought was funny. He smiled at me and patted me on the back. Nice man, I thought to myself.

"It was my job to get the machines working and I knew how. I knew how to work with the double-walled stainless cookers. I watched until the temperature gauges showed the milk to be at 146 degrees. After thirty minutes of that, I released the hot milk into the outside cooler. It cooled the milk down real fast.

"It was not hard to do if you knew how and I did.

"Mrs. Wallace had been working at her desk and then she called over the two men and gave them some tickets that they kept when they walked out of the door. I knew that they were going out in town knocking on doors and getting orders for milk. When closing time came they were back and gave the tickets back. In the meantime, I had poured up all of the cool milk into bottles and had them in refrigerators. Mr. Wallace came back, locked up the place and they all rode off. I went on home to our house up near the college.

"The same thing happened every day. Business was good. Lots of good milk. Lots of orders.

"One morning, about a month after we were working, Mr. Wallace stopped by me and asked me if I wanted to go down the street and get a cup of coffee with him. I quickly turned off my machine and we went out the door. I remember we walked up the hill and turned to our left and went down that side of the square for two or three blocks to a café that had a saw-dust floor.

"When we sat down and he ordered our coffee, Mr. Wallace dropped his head down low and said, quiet-like, to me, 'You know, I shouldn't have held that nigger's head down in that wash tub that long.'

"I was astonished. I had heard him. I didn't say anything.

"'No,' he repeated, 'I shouldn't have done that.' He seemed sad.

"'What happened to him?'

"'He drowned. No, I shouldn't have done that,' he repeated.

"After a long period of silence, we drank our coffee and walked back to the dairy. After that, I felt different about him. I often wondered if he told me the story about drowning the black man to let me know that he was 'in control.' But, I continued to work for him and he paid me on time every week.

"Then a bad thing happened about a year later. One morning when I got there, a policeman was waiting when we all showed up for work. He told Mr. Wallace that a colored woman had come to the police station and said that one of the men who worked there—there were four or five working there now—had jumped on her when she didn't *have the money to pay for the milk. The man said that she was talking about 'rape.' He told Mr. Wallace that he'd better get that place locked down and get all the workers back on home or there would be a big court case.*

"That was the last of Superior Dairy in LaGrange. Sometime later, Mr. Wallace got one of his buddies from down there to take over the place, a Mr. Guy Word. He changed the name from Superior Dairy to Word's Dairy but by then we had moved on to Montgomery."

Mr. Kenney often told that story during the many years he lived in Montgomery. He always ended the story by saying, "Working for Mr. John Wallace was something you never forgot."

*Right,
Josephine
Wallace as a
young woman.
Below, later
she would
work in a sock
factory.*

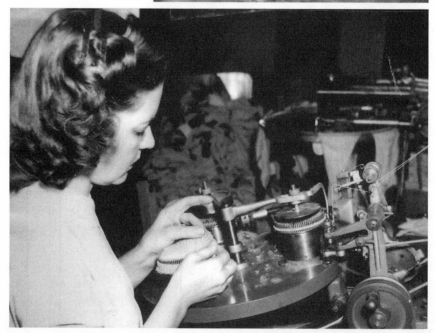

Whiskey stills.

President Franklin D. Roosevelt waving his hat from train car at Warm Springs, Georgia.

*Above, Howard Kenney
with prize cow.
Left, John Wallace and
friend.*

7

Going Around, Looking for Cows

"I would like to state that since 1936 of this time that I served,
that I have violated no laws that I am aware of. I have tried
to make a good citizen. I have worked hard for what I have."
— John Wallace

After the Superior Dairy debacle in LaGrange, John Wallace continued to live in his little house on Strickland Road with Josephine. His milk herd was successfully producing the golden milk that was gaining in popularity in the area surrounding his dairy farm. Josephine, and even one of her sisters, helped him by driving the pick-up, loaded with milk, to Columbus. Once, he helped a neighbor get his cows' milk accepted at the same dairy in Columbus.

During these years, Uncle Mozart stayed close to his house and was often quoted as saying, "All I want to do is raise a little cattle and enough corn for my cows and make a little corn liquor for myself and my friends." Myrtice sometimes went in to Chipley and to Warm Springs but she took off to Texas whenever she wanted to!

Uncles Eli and John Mercer Strickland were now dead, and as the reader can see, Mozart had never been inclined to assume a role of leadership, so now John Wallace was considered to be the unabashed leader of the Strickland family. But of what —"The Kingdom"? This title was sometimes used by authorities to describe the unusually large acreage of land which was now owned by John Wallace. However, no one around Meriwether County or Harris County has ever used the term.

Josephine, childless, was always unobtrusive. With the assistance of a helper, she saw that the meals were prepared according to John's liking and the house was kept neat and clean. His clothes were washed and hung outside when the weather was cooperative.

Unlike most of his neighbor men who wore overalls, John wore only heavy twill and denim pants and cotton shirts. Of course, like any gentleman dairy farmer, he had suits and ties to wear to funerals and to the banks and credit unions when he went to borrow money or to deposit milk and whiskey money. When he was outdoors, he wore a dress hat, jauntily perched on his head. Being completely bald and close-shaven, he always appeared neat and clean. He wore a signet ring, of unknown origin, on his left hand.

Josephine, ever pretty, had both talent and skill in her paintings which she exhibited to him and to his friends who came around the house when he was at home. She knew of an empty, unpainted wood building down at the end of Strickland Road where it ran into Highway 18, less than one from their house. Josephine asked John if she could have the building to show her paintings and the crafts which she made from scraps of materials that came her way.

John replied that, no, he had other plans for the building and, no, she could not use it. When "other plans" did not materialize and the building remained empty, she asked him again for the use of the building. This time, she later said, he did not even answer her. In less than a week, the wooden building burned to the ground.

When money was tight and he wanted to buy more land, he turned back to making liquor. His field hands, as he called them, were living on his place in two-room and three-room houses which had wells for water and "outhouses" for personal use. They did what he said, as did Josephine.

During these years of calmness he continued to go in and out of the house of his neighbors, the Dunlaps. Joe Dunlap had always lived near the Stricklands and was a friendly, smiling, impoverished farmer who once mortgaged his farm to Pope Davis for a little less than $400. To make ends meet, John's very dearest friend, Willie Carter Webb Dunlap, Joe's wife since 1914, often worked small jobs away from the farm. For instance, she worked in the cotton mill in West Point for a short while and once kept older women and men in a boarding house in Atlanta.

Daughter Dorothy went with her mother to these jobs even after she graduated from Young Harris College, which she attended reportedly at John's expense. Wherever they were, John found a way to visit Willie and Dorothy and to write them letters. Once, he wrote Dorothy, at her address in West Point where she and her mother were working at a textile mill, asking her not to tell Josephine that he was in Texas. He also asked Dorothy not to tell her mother that he loved her best, for he did. He went on to say, "I told Willie that I loved her best, too!" The bonds of John Wallace and Willie and Dorothy Dunlap were getting stronger and stronger as his attachment to Josephine shrank.

AFTER A LONG VISIT to Texas in the fall of 1940, Myrtice returned to her house not feeling well. Eventually doctors were consulted and it was disclosed that she had cancer. As ever, her beautiful and gracious daughter Jean came to the farm on the weekends (she was now the principal of an elementary school in Decatur, Georgia) to oversee the care of her mother. John did what a faithful son could do to make the days of Myrtice more comfortable.

Myrtice died on March 20, 1941.

MRS. MYRTICE WALLACE DIES

Mrs. Myrtice Wallace died last week at her home near White Sulphur Springs.

She was a member of the Methodist Church and a good and useful woman.

She leaves a son, Mr. John W. Wallace of White Sulphur Springs, a daughter, Mrs. Jean Mozley of Atlanta, and a brother, Mr. Mozart Strickland.

Funeral services were held at Hammett-Grover chapel after which her body was carried to West Point and interred by the side of her lamented husband.

The death of the good woman is the occasion of deep regret.

(Meriwether Vindicator. *Greenville, Georgia, March 28, 1941*)

John paid all the expenses of the funeral home and for the burial. Her will, as written on February 8, 1932 and witnessed by neighbors Charles Reid, Gladdice Mayo, and James H. Therrell, stated that daughter Jean was to be the executrix of the estate and her only heir. She left Jean all of her real estate and personal property, including the land in La Feria, Texas, with a total estimated value of $10,000.

If John was offended by the will, written one month after his wedding to Josephine Leath, he never said so.

8

Going for Broke

*"In '44 possibly, I had sold a good many hogs, and a Mr. Millard Rigsby from Carrollton came there and hauled the hogs away. I did not know who the driver was," — **John Wallace testimony, June 18, 1948***

The driver was William Turner. He had left the Army without leave and was then using his brother's name, Wilson. He had married into a good family originally from Heard County but was now living in Carroll County. Millard Rigsby, also from Carrollton, was a relative of Turner's wife. Though married a little more than two years and having a little baby boy, Turner's wife did not know that her husband's name was not Wilson.

When William Turner was on the Wallace farm, driving the truck to get the hogs, he had admired the beautiful, well-kept dairy farm. He saw the magnificent Guernsey cows slowly moving around in the pastures. He saw the squalid tenant houses, normal housing for tenants at that time and place. Turner also saw the nicer house where John Wallace and his wife lived. Then he saw another one that had been the first home that John Wallace had occupied with his mother when he returned from Young Harris College. Turner liked everything he saw.

Turner returned to the Wallace farm in late 1945 and asked for a job. After some negotiations, he and his wife, Julie, moved into the house that was once occupied by Myrtice and John. At first, according to John Wallace, the industrious young man worked so well that he was able to become a sharecropper. This arrangement gave him better opportunities than working in a cotton mill, which he had not liked. Turner told John Wallace that he wanted to work outside, not in a poorly ventilated mill where cotton lint hung in the air and which was hot in the summers and cold in the winters.

Turner was ambitious. He worked hard in his own vegetable garden and in his small cotton and corn field. Soon he learned how to help out at the whiskey still, a still which had been operated periodically by John Wallace for more than twenty years.

Wallace always insisted on telling his version of what happened to him beginning November 1, 1945. He once wrote a letter to William E. Wilburn, a new member of the Georgia Board of Pardons and Paroles. Wilburn had been appointed to the board six months after John's trial and perhaps Wallace was writing to give information he thought Wilburn might not have received:

Dear Mr. Wilburn,

Turner first moved on my farm about November 1, 1945 and worked by the day until spring of '46, then took a share-crop. I learned that he was a fugitive from Carroll County. He was tried in Carroll County for manufacturing whiskey and I helped him pay his fine. He made about $2,500 worth of cotton in 1946 and as lots of people do, immediately bought a car which was his undoing.

This got $1,250, half of his crop. He then prevailed on me to let him have a larger farm. I did. I let him have 100 acres—50 in cotton and 50 in corn and let him have a tractor outfit to operate it.

In March of 1947 I learned that he had resumed his liquor operations. I went to him and advised against the course of practice and tried to persuade him to discontinue the practice, but to no avail and later he was arrested and tried in Meriwether County Superior Court.

At that time I appealed to Judge Sam Boykin to have him moved out of Meriwether County. In his sentence he gave Turner a fine of $2,000 and twelve months in prison, suspended on condition that he leave Meriwether County. That was August, 1947. Judge Boykin allowed him 60 days to harvest his crops.

He then became involved in the liquor business on a larger scale than ever. On learning this . . . I talked with Mr. Roy Askew, my banker of Chipley, Georgia, and after this conversation, I went to Greenville to my attorney, Mr. Gus Huddleston. He called the Federal Department in Atlanta and asked that they send their agents down and destroy these operations.

These agents, Mr. Lucus and Mr. Bedenbaugh, who were stationed in Newnan, came to my house and I went with them and showed them his outfit. Later, the following day, they destroyed his place of operations but with no apparent effort to apprehend Turner. Later I called Mr. Miller of Woodland and advised him about the other operations, but each time Turner was allowed to go un-caught. Why? I cannot say.

I learned that Turner had enlisted the help of some of my colored tenants in his operation, so I called him and gave him specific orders to discontinue the practice. I went to Atlanta on that day and after my departure Turner, armed, followed the bus to LaGrange in an effort to avenge but missed me.

On learning of this condition, some of my friends appealed to the Sheriff of Meriwether County for protection for me as they had been advised that Turner planned to way-lay me at the train when I returned to Chipley on the night of the same day. When my train reached Greenville, the sheriff came to me from the train and drove me home in his personal car accompanied by his deputy, Mr. E. C. Perkerson. However Turner evidently cooled off and never made good his threats.

During the winter months of 1947–48 I had acquired a few head of dry cattle and had placed them on open range, having lots of swamp that had a profuse growth of honey-suckle. At intervals I would round them up and salt them.

On one occasion I found several head missing, about 20 in number. I searched high and low for the cattle never thinking that Turner was responsible but failing to locate these cattle, I drove the remaining cows home.

Then I missed a registered Guernsey cow and could find no trace of the cow and about 10 days later I missed two more; one that cost me $7,500 in S.C. and another that cost $250.

I can assure you at this point I was desperate. I called the sheriff who I had previously told about my losses and was trying to keep a watch on the herd to catch the thief. Mr. Collier and Mr. W. A. Biggers of Greenville came. They went to Montgomery, Alabama, to cover the sales houses. Mr. Sivell went to Macon, Mr. Smith of the G.B.I. [Georgia Bureau of Investigation] *went to Newnan and Atlanta and I went to Columbus, Buena Vista, Sylvester, Moultrie and Albany. Mr. Sivell and I went back to Atlanta and covered the Ragsdale-Lawhorn sale. I went to Rome to the auction sale.*

On reaching Chipley that night on my return home I was advised that one of my cows had been located in Carrollton. I immediately returned to Carrollton, identified the cow, and kept a watch to find whoever the thief was. It was then that I became convinced that Turner was responsible. I watched this cow Wednesday, Thursday, Friday and Saturday nights, never once going to bed during that time and on Sunday night, Mr. Threadgill, chief of police in Carrollton, caught Turner about 7:00 pm in the act of getting the cow. I reached Carrollton about 9:00 pm. We found the cow at 1:00 am.

I reached home about sunrise, Monday am. This was 7 days and 8 nights that I'd been on the trail of these cattle. I was about dead on my feet. About 9:30 pm Monday night, Mr. Collier came to my house and advised me that Mr. Wyatt, the solicitor of my district, had told him that he would have to release Turner and prosecute him in Carroll County.

Knowing of my previous experience with Turner when he was riled with me, the sheriff told me to move my bed away from a window . . . that Turner might shoot me while I slept in bed when and after he was released from Meriwether County jail.

However on leaving, he told me to come to Greenville the following morning which was April 20, 1948. I went there as he suggested and when I reached there, it

*was decided that I should go back home and get help and intercept Turner and gain
a confession from him with enough evidence to hold him—for trial in Meriwether
County—and also be able to recover the remaining cattle or return from wherever
they had been sold.*

John Wallace's letter continued on with his version of what happened later that
day, which included the incident that occasioned the murder trial that would begin
June 14, 1948.

*After intercepting Turner at the Sunset Tourist Camp which was about forty
miles from Atlanta, I returned him to the premises where he took my cattle. I was
anxious to get the details about his operations . . . and had no intention to take his
life and when the gun accidentally fired, I did not know he had been struck until I
turned around and found him dead. His scalp was blown off and had the gun had
even an inch more acceleration, he would have never been struck.*

Turner was dead, he admitted.

In that long letter that Wallace sent to Wilburn, he added that Sheriff Collier
told him to "forget that I had ever seen Turner," which, according to John Wallace,
"didn't suit me," but, with the ordeal that he had been through in the past nine days
looking for his cattle, "my mind as well as my body was about shot."

He then ended his letter after sending appropriate good wishes and asking Wilburn
to show the letter to Governor Talmadge, which Wilburn probably did not do.

9

Going to Moreland

"A rumor spread throughout Meriwether and Harris counties that Potts was determined to get even with Sheriff Collier of Meriwether County, for the latter had once killed the former's nephew." — **Name Withheld**

It was true that on April 12 John Wallace had reported the theft of two of his cows and six days later, on April 18, Turner was caught attempting to move one stolen cow from a Carrollton pasture.

On April 18 or 19 (the record is not clear), Turner was taken from the jail in Carrollton and delivered to the Meriwether County Jail. His pick-up truck was also transported to Greenville by one of the deputies. At noon on the 20th, when he was released, Turner saw that John Wallace and his friends were watching and waiting for him. He jumped in his vehicle and took off! A story in A. L. Henson's book, *Confessions of a Criminal Lawyer*, states that all of those involved, including William Turner, had lunch together in the Meriwether County Jail as guests of Sheriff Hardy Collier. Not likely.

At any rate, it is known that Turner raced toward Newnan but ran out of gas just as he came to the Sunset Motel, which had a small café attached. Significantly, Sunset was just inside the county line of Coweta County, whose chief law enforcement officer was Sheriff Lamar Potts.

Turner jumped out of his truck and ran toward the café. He was caught just as he reached the door by both Wallace and his friend, Herring Sivell, who had hesitatingly come with him on this ill-fated mission. They caught Turner by his arms and attempted to push and pull Turner back into Sivell's car. When Turner resisted, Wallace hit him in the head with the butt of a shotgun, then shoved him into the back seat of Sivell's car. Several people watched the altercation.

Therein rests the case that determined the eventual outcome of John Wallace's life.

Later in the court trial, two witnesses would testify that they saw Turner being killed right there in Coweta County at the motel's café and that someone rushed out and shouted at Wallace and Sivell, asking them to be more gentle with the fellow. One man testified that he saw it all but "just kept on eating."

Wallace testified that the blow made only a cut on Turner's head. Sivell gave a deposition stating that Turner was hurt, but not badly. Investigations showed that he bled profusely.

John Wallace and Sivell jumped into Sivell's car, and with Turner lying on the floor of the back seat, they headed back to Greenville. Only a few miles down the road, Sivell sensed that one of his tires was going flat. Fortunately, the other car, driven by Henry Mobley, had intercepted them, had turned around and was following. The two cars pulled over to the right side of the highway.

Sivell said that Turner walked over to the Mobley car and, unassisted, again got in the back seat. Sivell said he stood by the roadside and watched as the Mobley car proceeded south with John Wallace, William Turner, and Tom Strickland in the car with Henry Mobley driving. Sivell never saw them again that fateful day.

Sivell repaired his flat tire and went home to Chipley. When he got there, he told his wife, "Well, John did get mad and I think he got us into some big trouble, even though he promised us he was not going to do that." "Big trouble," he repeated.

Somehow, it is not clear how, Sheriff Potts heard from one of the café witnesses that John Wallace and Herring Sivell had been seen at the tourist camp and that there was a violent struggle with a slight, young, white man. A day later Turner's distraught wife reported that her husband was missing.

On April 27, a massive search began for Turner. With radio and newspaper announcements, requests for help to find Turner were made. Countless volunteers responded and were soon available for the search—one newspaper reported that two hundred men were out looking for Turner. Law enforcement officers came from several surrounding counties, including the sheriff of Muscogee County and his staff from the Columbus area; the Georgia Highway Patrol joined the search, as well as agents of the State Bureau of Revenue. Each morning Sheriff Potts stood on the top step at the front door of the Coweta County Courthouse and gave specific instructions for the day's search.

During this same period, when receiving no help from ailing Sheriff Hardy Collier of Meriwether County, Sheriff Potts called Wallace and asked him to come in with Sivell, just to talk with him about the missing William Turner. With attorney Gus Huddleston at their sides, the two men entered the Newnan courthouse to talk.

Instead, Sheriff Potts clasped handcuffs on Wallace and Sivell. A loud outcry came from Wallace. Nevertheless, the two men were pushed into a jail cell and charged with "kidnapping." The charge was not murder, because, in Georgia at that time, the law of *corpus delicti* prevailed: no body, no murder.

Each morning after that, Wallace watched though the window of his cell at the jail house as the posse, as it was being called, left Newnan heading toward Meriwether County, looking for Turner.

Wallace knew they would not find Turner, of course.

He had burned him up!

Left, Turner was accused of stealing Wallace's cows. After Turner was released from the Meriwether County jail, he sped off toward Newnan. But he was intercepted by Wallace. Below, the grappling hook.

WLLIAM TURNER, alias Wilson Turner, who was last seen Tuesday afternoon, just after noon, at the Sunset Tourist Camp, where he was reportedly assaulted by two men, thrown into the rear of a green tudor Ford, and carried away in a southward direction on Highway 41, presumably heading toward Greenville. $500 reward for information leading to his recovery.

Meriwether County Jail, Greenville, Georgia, where Turner was being held.

Above, John Wallace with his wife, Josephine, and her father, Judge Leath. Right, Coweta County Sheriff Lamar Potts, intently studying a match box. In the movie, Potts would be played by Johnny Cash.

Above, the jail in Newnan where John Wallace was kept after his arrest for Turner's murder. Opposite page, Wallace's jail cell.

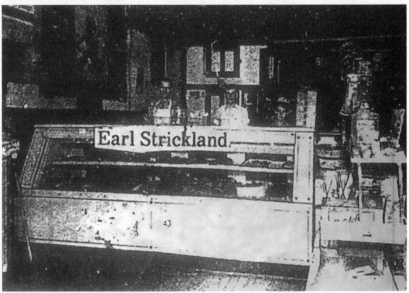

Above, the train depot in Newnan. Right, Strickland's Market, where Wallace placed orders while he was jailed in Newnan.

STRICKLAND MARKET
17 East Broad Street in Newnan

To Mr. & Mrs Strickland and Employes

Please accept these little gifts as a token of appreciation of the kind attitude and sympathetic acts shown me since Ive been at the jail —

Sincerely —

John Wallace

Mr & Mrs Strickland
Joe Burnham
Lamar Story
Mr. Hinsley
size Short (?)
Pr. wool Socks
for the men
and a nice
Handkuchief for
Mrs Strickland

Sunday night —

Dearest Dottie —

Who should come in yesterday about 3:00 P.M. but Mrs. Wallace. She said that she just decided to come see what had happened to me. Mr. Potts came down and let her in and she left at 7:00 on the train for Shipley. She spent the night with "Min-Ha" and came back up this A.M. and left tonight back to Shipley —

She plans to go to Columbus to-morrow to try and get employment. Don't know how she will come out. Says that she is going to see Pijie Goter who works with a real estate Co also was going to contact Dr. Ganny.

She had only 16-17 ¢ ... I told her the only thing I ca... down to Gapo is sh... see what she cd it ... want to

90 34 E 131 St. ... may go Newnan, Ga. ... Come this,

Miss Dorothy Dunlap
Shipley, Ga.

... will go to Newnan ... Dr. Lips
... Wednesday ... me by the fence. They
... Henry was the worst lie-
... he ever saw.

Wallace wrote this letter to Dorothy Dunlap while he was in the jail in Newnan, Georgia.

A historical view of the courthouse square in Coweta County, Newnan, Georgia.

10

Going to Trial

"Somebody planted those clothes." — *John **Wallace, writing in his Bible, November 1, 1950***

While the search for William Turner was going on, Sheriff Lamar Potts and a deputy went uninvited to White Sulphur Springs to the home of John Wallace, who was then languishing in his jail cell in Newnan. Josephine was home alone. When she was told that the visitors needed to search the house, she, with great charm, invited them inside and conducted a tour throughout the small, neat house. In the back hall, Sheriff Potts spied a wicker laundry basket filled to the brim with dirty clothes. He asked permission to go through them. She readily agreed, somewhat apologizing that there were so many dirty clothes, but "wash day," she stated, was only two days away.

In the basket, Potts found a pair of pants and a shirt with what appeared to be blood on them. He then asked permission to take the pants and shirt with him. Again, she agreed, amicably. Later, Dr. Herman Jones, Fulton County's "crime doctor," said the spots found on Wallace's clothing were human blood. If Dr. Jones had located a matching blood type from Turner's Army records, he perhaps would have been very close to declaring it to be Turner's blood.

It was also during this time that someone, possibly a neighbor, reported in a se-cretive telephone call that Turner had been cremated at a former whiskey still site. A loud boom had been heard by neighbors over a distance of several miles. A fire had consumed brush and small trees for a swath of forty feet, and trees were burned to a height of sixty feet. It seems strange that the large group of men who were searching the forests could have missed the signs of such a massive fire, but they did. Or they simply made no connection between the burn site and the missing Turner.

The caller requested a private meeting to give further details of the cremation. Farmhand helpers Albert Brooks and Robert Lee Gates later confirmed the fire when confronted by Sheriff Potts. They also told of being told to search for "a package" which was in reality Turner's body. Wallace insisted that they use a large grappling hook to reach down into the many abandoned wells on his farms. Eventually, after a day-long search, the grappling hook snagged the body and Gates and Brooks tugged and pulled until the body of William Turner came out of the well and tumbled onto the ground. It was then that the large fire was made and the body was burned.

However, the story told in the newspapers of the fire consuming Turner's body overnight could not be accurate. According to medical forensic scientists, "No fire, not even with gallons and gallons of explosive gasoline, could have consumed the body overnight! To cremate a body requires a constant temperature of at least 1,100 degrees. Tissue could have been consumed overnight but a total body would have required 3-4 DAYS of burning and with continuous dousing of gasoline." Did anyone do that? Or could larger bones have been buried somewhere? "Teeny, tiny bones could have been burned and would have floated in the nearby stream," reported the authority on cremation.

A thorough search of the area probably would have located a makeshift burial site.

After the trial was over, or so the story goes, the confidential caller received a cash reward of five hundred dollars, provided by Potts and delivered by Elzie Hancock. The person who received the reward was not identified by Hancock or Potts in their lifetimes. The "woodsman," as the person was called in Margaret Anne Barnes's book,

Murder in Coweta County, is now sometimes thought to be a woman, not a man. However, there are some who insist that there never was a "woodsman" and that Tom Strickland told the sheriff about the fire in a confession given in the Newnan jail. Time has not told.

WITHOUT THE BONE SHARDS that were presented in court as the body of William Turner, John Wallace could have never been charged with murder. Remember *corpus delicti?* With his own confession that he accidentally shot Turner, he probably would have been charged with manslaughter.

But when the floating bone shards were discovered in a small creek, Judge Samuel Boykin wasted little time in calling for a grand jury to consider the charges. The grand jury indicted seven men on murder charges. The defendants included Meriwether County Sheriff Collier as an accessory to murder.

The trial would begin on June 14, 1948, less than two months from the date Turner was killed.

Some days after the bone shards (which were placed in a matchbox) were recovered, federal revenue agents announced they had broken one of the largest liquor rings in Georgia. The distillery was on John Wallace's land. Warrants were issued for John Wallace, who was in jail, William Turner, who was dead, Albert Brooks and Robert Lee Gates, who were hidden away, and several unnamed farm workers. The announcement could not have helped Wallace in his upcoming trial, nor in the long speech that he would foolishly give on the last day of the trial.

In the past when there had been a legal problem or just a need for advice, Wallace had turned to lawyer Gus Huddleston of Greenville. However, as his trial date neared, Wallace was urged to get a lawyer with more experience in the courtroom. A. L. Henson of the Atlanta law firm of Harris, Henson, Spence, and Gower was just the man. Henson later wrote:

"I was associated in the case two weeks before it was to be tried. When I arrived in Newnan, it was a very hot June day in 1948. I had to drive around the crowds which

were milling about the courthouse ground and park on the outskirts of town. The paved streets and sidewalks had already absorbed enough from the sun to be oppressive. Little concession stands were on every corner, serving the crowd with soft drinks and hot dogs."

ON JUNE 14TH, A large crowd of those involved in the trial—friends of John Wallace, his family, including Josephine and her father—and curious spectators gathered in Newnan. Word had been spread by newspapers, radio, and by word-of-mouth that the rich man was going to be tried for killing a poor tenant farmer.

John Wallace was not wealthy. Though he owned large tracts of land, much of the land was mortgaged; he owed everybody. Regardless, newspapers and radio station broadcasters continued to restate the adjective "wealthy" whenever his name was mentioned. And little boys sold tickets for seats in the courtroom.

The "Burned Bones" trial was about to begin, and its upcoming date was being broadcast and written about across the Southern states, particularly in Georgia and Alabama. On the day the trial began, lawyer Huddleston compared the temperament of the crowd to that of the crowd which had gathered on July 28, 1913, in Atlanta for the trial of Leo Frank for killing Mary Phagan. Yet Turner was a convicted felon, while Mary Phagan was a dear little girl who worked in a pencil factory and made the mistake of going for her meager paycheck on a Saturday morning when a drunken janitor lurked in the basement of the building. The Wallace case should have seemed very different.

Soon Henson learned that the potential jurors had not even been summoned by the procedure required by Georgia law; the men—only white men were eligible for jury service—had merely received a postal card from the sheriff telling them to appear. And when questioned about any personal bias about employing capital punishment, not one of the 109 white men, primarily farmers, asked to be excused for that reason. "Never before had I witnessed a call of jurors in a capital felony case where at least ten percent were [not] disqualified for that reason, and I have seen it go as high as fifty per cent," said Henson. The twelve jurors eventually selected apparently had no misgivings over the potential use of the electric chair as punishment for John Wallace.

Sheriff Potts had also advertised over the radio that there was reward money for information. Henson, referring to the improper jury notification and the sheriff's personal use of reward money, objected, saying, "Because of his personal interest in the case he was disqualified to serve and to summon said jury." Judge Boykin disregarded Henson's first objection. There would be several more objections during the course of the five-day trial. All were denied.

THE TRIAL BEGAN. Two major witnesses to the assault were called. They were positive that they had seen John Wallace kill William Turner. They were certain that Turner was killed upon contact. Certain. Two doctors stated that their testimony was accurate, even though one witness was standing across the road, a hundred yards away, when Turner was struck and the other witness was inside a small café overlooking the parking places. "Certain," they said.

The trial continued.

Next, Henson was astonished when he saw Robert Lee Gates and Albert Brooks brought into the courtroom. They had been hidden in a Columbus, Georgia, jail until that day. Wallace's attorneys had been given no opportunity to question the two black men before the trial began, and Henson had never even heard of them before they were escorted into the courtroom.

However, Henson was required to move ahead with the trial. He asked each of the men the same questions and got the same answers:

"Have you talked with anyone except Sheriff Potts since he took you off?"

"No, sir."

"He told you what to do and say?"

"Yes, sir."

"And that is what you are doing and saying?"

"Yes, sir."

That black men had openly testified in a courtroom in Georgia caused the trial to be known as "the first trial where a white man was convicted because of the words of a 'colored' man."

Mayhayley Lancaster, the well-known fortune-teller, was next sworn in and was asked about John Wallace's coming to her house for help in finding his cows and then returning to ask her the whereabouts of a body that was lost.

State Patrolman J. C. Otwell later said that he was surprised to hear her testify that she had told Wallace, "His body is in a well, covered in flies," as had been reported in the newspapers.

In fact, Otwell said that when he and Agent Jim Hillin went to see her, sent by prosecutor Luther Wyatt, "She told us that, yes, Wallace did come to see her and, yes, she told us that she told him that the body he was looking for was in the Chattahoochee River!" When the well was located that had once held Turner's body, it was Otwell who went down into the well and then to Mayhayley's disingenuous testimony, he added, "That well was far too deep for any flies!" She had changed her story to please the prosecutors, according to Otwell.

The trial of John Wallace was becoming a sham.

However, the following day, June 17th, the *Atlanta Journal* reported:

> *Miss Mayhayley Lancaster, seer known to thousands in this area, at times has attracted almost as much attention in the trial of John Wallace for murder as the defendant himself. Particularly, when she testified that Wallace asked her if the body of William Turner would be found and she told him, 'It certainly will.'*

And so it went.

But the startling turn of events was when the three men who had been with John Wallace on April 20 and were his only witnesses refused to testify in his defense. They had been assured by the prosecutors, "If you refuse to testify *for* Wallace, we will see that you do not go to the electric chair." And at that time, as this trial was going, it seemed rather certain that Wallace would be found guilty and would be sentenced to die in Georgia's electric chair.

It is understandable that Henry Mobley, Herring Sivell, and Tom Strickland would not want to be electrocuted for going with John Wallace to apprehend Turner in order to discover where Wallace's missing cows were hidden or were being sold! While it was true that Sivell had been with Wallace when Turner was apprehended, the other two, Mobley and Strickland, were not even at the Sunset Tourist Camp (they were late) but they had been earlier seen in Greenville before the chase began! For this, Mobley and Strickland would receive life sentences to be endured in a Georgia prison. However, they had also been quietly told that a life sentence in Georgia at that time would be for only eight years, assuming this was their first offense.

On the last day of the trial when Wallace's only witnesses had refused to testify, several of his attorneys suggested that Wallace, himself, should testify. Lead attorney Henson opposed this idea, believing that Wallace might say things that would make him appear even more guilty. He was right. The other lawyers (there were five, by then) disagreed with Henson, so John Wallace marched to the witness chair, calmly sat down, and for seven hours he talked and talked. Naturally, the audience was spellbound.

John Wallace began by telling his life story in great detail. Although there were significant episodes omitted, like his marriage to Josephine, his uncles' murders, and the death of his parents, it was a true story. The crowd in the courtroom sat silently and politely listened, as did Judge Boykin, the attorneys for both sides, and all of the law enforcement officers.

When he came to the end of his story, the assembled were still waiting to hear about the body being burned, but John Wallace just said that after shooting Turner, by accident, his mind "just went blank." He could not remember anything further, he said.

When John Wallace said that his "mind just went blank" there was a rustle heard in the courtroom as many of the assembled shifted in their seats, clasped their hands over their mouths and "air was sucked out." Unbelievable! Shocked! Startled! Many of the people had been sitting in the Coweta County Courthouse since Monday, June 14th, to hear about the "burned bones."

The only people in the room who believed him were his friends, and some of them may have been doubtful.

The crowd and even the jury probably would have forgiven him for the murder, for murders and killings were fairly common (especially when the victim was black, though Turner of course was not). Mayhayley Lancaster, the most colorful addition to the trial, often advised her customers when wrongdoings were reported to her down in her ancient log cabin in nearby Heard County, to "Just go on home and settle it yourselves." They often did.

It was the burning of Turner's body that was not forgivable. John Wallace was seeking to escape charges of murder by getting rid of his victim. Whether Turner had been killed in Newnan as some said, intentionally shot in the Meriwether County woods, or accidentally shot as Wallace testified, *corpus delicti* ruled his decision.

Then and now in that part of the country, the body of a deceased person is treated with sentiment and respect, and religious funerals are usually held. A funeral, preceded by food and adorned by flowers, will draw family and friends from far and near. But on June 18th when the trial was over, the mood of the jury, and of most of the crowd, was outrage. "An eye for an eye and a tooth for a tooth" was a Bible verse that most knew and many had been raised to believe. John Wallace's "mind going blank" would determine the decision of the jury. He should have listened to Henson and never gotten on the witness stand!

"The jury went out about three o'clock in the afternoon," recalled Henson. "I thought I would go to my hotel, half a block away, and pack my bag so I could leave promptly when the verdict was in. As I walked into the lobby, the hotel clerk and the few people standing about were congratulating the county on the verdict—the electric chair. The verdict had been returned and the judge had entered sentence before I could walk half a block to the hotel."

The jury had not believed the ending of Wallace's seven-hour speech. One would never forget a massive fire and the burning of a dead body.

The trial of John Wallace was over.

Above, courtroom scene during Wallace's trial.
Left, Wallace during the proceedings.

Another scene during the trial, with Wallace in the center.

Above, Sivell, Mobley, and Strickland in the courthouse during a break. Right, the eccentric Mayhayley Lancaster. Below, William Turner's father and brother.

Sheriff Potts, right, and an unidentified man examine some of the evidence in the case.

11

Going for Lawyer Money

"To said Party, J.P. Davis of Harris County for six thousand dollars ($6,000), John Wallace of Meriwether County does hereby convey the following properties . . ." — **wrote Attorney Gus Huddleston, June 26, 1948**

When John Wallace heard the guilty sentence on late Friday afternoon, June 18, 1948, among his immediate problems—aside from his possible death in two months—was that he knew that he had no money; he was broke. He had hired five lawyers. His land was mortgaged to the hilt to the Greenville Production Credit Association, Farmers and Merchants Bank, Federal Land Bank of Columbus, Georgia, and to the Citizens and Southern Bank of LaGrange. He also owed money to the Wisdom Motor Company and to individuals (Henry Zackry and Charles Harman).

He had recently invested heavily in the milk cows. As he said more than once, he had paid $3,200 (he said he had paid $7,200 in a letter to Paroles Board member, Wilburn, an honest mistake on his part) for just one registered Guernsey, and almost as much for another cow. Unlike the publicity that surrounded him, he was far from being a "wealthy Meriwether County farmer" but was an impoverished dairyman whose expensive cows were being stolen. He had found only one—cut from ear to ear—left rotting in his woods.

Perhaps more important, Turner's extravagant living style had disrupted the real source of Wallace's income: the whiskey-making business. Turner was riskily making corn liquor with the help of Wallace's farm laborers. Turner had commandeered Wallace's whiskey-making enterprise, the one that the Strickland uncles had developed more than thirty years before. Not only was the source of his income dried up, but most assuredly, Wallace was scared that Turner would implicate him when he was caught. After all, John Wallace believed he was still on probation from his last offense. He had been very careful up until now.

Turner had bought himself a 1942 Super Deluxe pickup truck on December 23, 1946, from LaGrange Motors, paying $750 down and committing to monthly payment of $54.67, which included insurance and finance charges, for the next two years. To infuriate Wallace further, Turner had also talked one of Wallace's longtime field hands into buying a vehicle, too. Wallace said he watched them as they rode up and down the roads, "And on my time," Wallace declared.

On Friday afternoon, June 18th, when he calmly but unsmilingly walked to the jail with Sergeant J. C. Otwell beside him, Wallace decided to do the only thing he could: sell out!

He immediately contacted Gus Huddleston and had him draw up a two-page list of properties which he would turn over to Pope Davis, who was his closest friend, the best man in his wedding, and his second cousin, once-removed, with whom he shared a common great-granddaddy, Eli Davis. Lawyer Huddleston completed the legal work by the following Saturday, the 26th of June.

For $6,000, Pope was to receive many separate tracts of land: 199.4 acres of land; 101.25 acres of land; a tract of 5 acres; 67.55 acres; 46.7 acres of land; lot 146 with 202.5 acres; a tract with 40 acres; 113 acres; 281 acres which had been the original Strickland home place; 252.5 acres; 86 acres; 97.5 acres; "Hasty Warehouse," a two-story brick building in Chipley with an adjoining empty lot; lots 1–7, 11, and 12 of the Charles Harman property southeast of LaGrange; an 8-acre parcel in the town of Stovall; lots 6–12 within the town of Stovall; and one more 7.2 acre piece of property near his house.

Two days later, June 28th, Wallace assigned to Pope 218.2 more acres located at the confluence of Strickland and Chipley roads. He had bought this land in February 1921, soon after he returned to the little house where he lived with his mother. It was mortgaged to the Federal Land Bank in Columbus. Pope purportedly gave him $1,275 for the land. His cousin, F. Kiser Whatley Jr., was his attorney and his friend Holmes Clements was the notary public who witnessed their signatures.

In all probability, no money was exchanged between Pope Davis and John Wallace, only a handshake between best friends.

When John Wallace later told a newspaper reporter, "I don't have a stick of land, nor a penny to my name, and I am not afraid to die," he was telling the truth about the land, for he had transferred it to Pope Davis. However, most of his land was subject to mortgages. Pope Davis would oversee the land holdings and would attempt to remove the liens over the next seven years.

LESS THAN A WEEK later, July 13th, several hundred potential buyers and sightseers came to his farm on Strickland Road for a widely advertised auction. They were probably not aware that John Wallace's friend, Meriwether County Sheriff Hardy Collier had died that same week. In spite of the drained lake filled with stinking dead fish, the enthusiastic buyers purchased everything: the mules, the horses, a donkey, the tractors, the farm implements, and his treasured milk cows. Someone even bought his spotted cat! He only kept the small house and its immediate adjoining land.

Standing by Josephine's father, Judge John Leath, on the front porch of the little Wallace house while the rowdy auction was going on was a prominent educator from the area, who later related that Judge Leath strolled over to him and asked, in a quiet, confidential manner, "See that screen door?"

The educator looked in the direction that Judge Leath was pointing. "Yes, I see that screen door," he replied.

"John Wallace threw my daughter right through it."

His listener quickly replied, "Nobody would throw my daughter through a screen door and live to tell it!"

Judge Leath only frowned, said nothing, turned away and went into the house where everyone suspected that Josephine was inside, hiding.

At the end of the day, the auctioneer announced that $17,000 had been gained from the auction. That amount would appear to be enough money to pay old debts, the five lawyers, and the court costs, and still leave some for future bills. However, the money did not last long enough for optimistic John Wallace. No one suspected that the appeals would continue for two years, six months, and twenty-three days after the tragic affair at Moreland, the site of the motel and cafe.

Wallace was like his father who had owed so many, and also like his father, he had many friends who would do *anything* for him. The story is often told that Buddy Hart, a confirmed bachelor of nearby Mountville, was known to carry large sums of money on his person. On the eve of the Wallace trial, Mr. Hart was approached by two men in his little store and asked for help with their automobile. It was closing time at his store, so he agreed, and asked the two men to follow him to his nearby house where he had some tools. The men followed him to the house where he lived with his elderly parents. Buddy Hart briefly went inside and told his parents that he was outside helping some men with their car. Those were his last words.

After he went back outside, his parents heard one shot and then they heard a car rush away, moving toward Greenville. They found their son, Buddy Hart, dead in their front yard. His money was gone.

One member of the family has told over and over that the robbery was done by Wallace's friends helping him in the expenses of his trial. There is no evidence that Buddy Hart's robbery and murder were related to John Wallace; it is just an oft-told story. Yet, the Buddy Hart murder is one of the very few unsolved crimes in Troup County, Georgia.

OTHER THAN DEALING WITH his financial problems, John Wallace had many visitors:

old men friends, Willie and Dorothy Dunlap and Josephine. On some occasions he was even allowed to walk freely around downtown Newnan. He was soon shopping in Strickland's Market.

Two months after his incarceration, he wrote:

8/28/48

To Mr. and Mrs. Strickland and Employees,

 Please accept these little gifts as a token of appreciation of the kind attitude and sympathetic acts shown me since I've been at the jail.

 Sincerely,

John Wallace

 Pair of nice socks for the men: Mr. Strickland, Joe Burnham, Lamar Story and Mr. Hensley (size about 11) and a nice handkerchief for Mrs. Strickland.

A drug store in Newnan had been enlisted to take his lunch to him every day for he was not happy with the food being supplied in the jail. He had an open charge account at the drug store to pay for his meals and cigarettes.

When he did not have friends, lawyers, or relatives visiting him, Sheriff Potts dropped in to talk and listen. On one occasion he told the sheriff that he had killed four men in his life. "They all needed it," he explained.

In his spare time, he wrote letters.

Only three days after the auction, July 17th, he wrote Mr. Robert C. Key, a banker of LaGrange;

Dear Mr. Bob,

 I am writing you to say a few things about Tom Strickland.

 Now, Mr. Bob this world is a sad place for we fellows who were involved.

 However the facts which were used of the things used against us never happened in Coweta County or anywhere else.

 I know because I know everything that did happen. So does Tom know everything that happened on the day up to the death of Turner. Further than that, he knew nothing and at no time did Tom do anything to injure Turner nor did he know in advance anything was going to happen to his life—not even one second before he was killed.

He is innocent of the charge of murder in this county and is innocent of any act that caused Turner's death and he should be at home if he had justice.

In fact, if justice had been done in this county we all would be home now. The man was not killed here neither was he injured except a small cut on the ear which he himself mentioned was of no consequence.

I have no motive for writing you this except that I'm sure you are especially concerned about Tom and I want you to know that he is innocent of the crime and should never have served a minute, much less life.

This comes from one who knows all there is to know about the case.

With kindest regard for you and your dear wife,

Sincerely yours,

Jno Wallace

To Tom Strickland, he wrote:

Dear Tom,

I know of no news but I thought I'd tell you that I wrote Mr. Bob Key last week and told him that you were innocent of anything in the death of Turner so that maybe he would have a statement from one who knows all there is to know about it. Possibly he can be of some help to you at the proper time.

I trust that you all won't have to stay down there long. It is a terrible thing to have to serve time for something that never even happened. But that's what you all are doing.

I hope I can see you all sometime. However, I don't know anything.

Sincerely,

John Wallace

John often underlined parts of his letters. He also sometimes signed his name as "Jno," other times as "John," especially to those who were more familiar to him, like Dorothy, Willie, and his beloved sister, Jean.

John had written to Tom Strickland, probably because he was kin, a first cousin, once-removed. Tom's father, Solomon, was the brother of Zeke Strickland, John's grandfather. Tom was a decorated, seriously wounded soldier from the First World War, and his wife and granddaughter, both named Maidee, had suffered troubling deaths. However, he was admired in the community for he "kept" his brother, Frank, until Frank died. Frank was deaf and mute (Census records denote "deaf and dumb," because that is what *dumb* means, not *stupid*.)

Letters to John Wallace usually kept his spirits up. A letter from one of his very oldest friends who once lived near him in White Sulphur Springs but now in La Feria was more realistic. He wrote, "I understand you are to get a new hearing concerning a new trial the 12th of this month. Hope you have better luck than you have had in the past." He added, "We made a good crop of cotton, 254 bales," which probably did not make John feel any better now that he had lost everything.

His attorneys were busy. Henson appealed for a new trial on June 21, only two days after the sentence was first given by Judge Boykin. It was turned down nearly two months later, on August 18th. Another appeal was made to the Georgia Supreme Court on October 2nd. Henson asked for a new trial on November 17th. On New Year's Day, January 1, 1949, the Georgia Supreme Court upheld the Coweta County verdict and denied a new trial. Henson and Huddleston requested a new trial in the United States District Court.

Regardless, John Wallace's execution was rescheduled for February 11th at 2 P.M. An appeal was made to the Georgia Pardons and Paroles Board to commute the death sentence to life imprisonment. Newly elected Governor Herman Talmadge granted a thirty-day stay at the request of the board. Then the Georgia Pardons and Paroles Board announced that a public hearing would be granted and set it for February 24, 1949.

THE APPEAL TO THE members of the Georgia Pardons and Paroles Board was so well publicized that a crowd gathered so large that the hearing had to be moved from their board room to the auditorium of the Georgia legislature. One newspaper said that seventy-five people were there; another said "several hundred." His family and friends had come from Meriwether County and from all over Harris County. They came from LaGrange, West Point, and from Chambers County, Alabama.

Wallace was moved from the Newnan jail to Atlanta and sat silently and listened— he was not allowed speak—as they spoke, not of his innocence, but of their wishes that his death sentence could be commuted to life imprisonment. At that time, the attorneys had given up on a new trial to be held back home in Meriwether County. "Just don't kill him," they begged.

Young Helen Hammett, whom he had befriended in Santa Rosa and La Feria, Texas, came from Young Harris College and when called upon, she quietly told of his many acts of kindness to her and concluded with, "He is like a father to me."

Presbyterian minister H. G. Harry, who held churches in Manchester and in Greenville, spoke eloquently of John's kindness to so many, in spite of a childhood "that left him an orphan" and "uncles who brutalized him and forced him into bootlegging." The Atlanta newspapers covered the hearing but never refuted the testimony, for in truth his uncle Mozart loved him dearly and his mother would have never allowed anyone to harm him in any way. Other than the death of his parents and his bout with the Spanish Flu, he had lived a charmed *early* life.

In a most unusual occurrence, on Tuesday, March 1st, the famed editor of the *Atlanta Consitution*, Ralph McGill, headed the editorial page with:

IT'S THE LAW THAT IS ON TRIAL

This is a difficult editorial to write. It is difficult because it must, to a sense, deal with a specific case and involves the emotions of those interested. It is difficult, too, because we are not all convinced that capital punishment is the deterrent for which it was instituted. This, however, is beside the point. It is the present law.

There is before the State Pardons and Paroles Board the case of John Wallace of

Meriwether County. We do not know the defendant. We have no personal feelings whatsoever either for or against him. We wish it were possible to discuss the issue without mentioning him or his case. It is not so possible. This we sincerely regret.

He was convicted of one of the most brutal and horribly cruel murders in the history of the state. The appeals courts including the Supreme Court have sustained the verdict of the jury. No new evidence has been presented.

Both Wallace and the man murdered had previous criminal records. Wallace is a man of wealth and reportedly has friends with political influence.

The case, or any similar case, puts the State and the Paroles Board on trial.

Is capital punishment, and the verdict of a jury, sustained by all the courts and unchanged by new evidence, reserved in Georgia for Negroes and poor whites? Is it to be the lot of the obscure and friendless who do not have money or influence?

We intend here to express merely an opinion; we are not attempting to recommend a course of action in this specific case.

But if the defendant in this awful and violent murder case is to be relieved of the jury's decision, then at the same time we urge the Board to commute the sentence of every person now under the death sentence—not one of them has been found more guilty than Wallace—and notify the juries of the state that all future death sentences will be commuted.

To ADD TO WALLACE's financial problems, on March 19th the widow of William Turner was awarded $7,000 for damages, based on Turner's life expectancy. She had sued John Wallace and his three compatriots for $74,280.

Wallace's latest appeal was turned down April 18, 1949, perhaps in part due to Ralph McGill's editorial. Then, the court resentenced Wallace to die on May 6, 1949.

There would be more electrocution dates announced, more delays and more appeals. John Wallace would be "in limbo," but alive, for two and a half years.

12

Going for Acquittal or Life Sentence

*"John Wallace is my only brother. It is my belief that he is
the victim of perjured testimony and a grossly mismanaged
defense." — **wrote Jean, February 14, 1949***

T he lawyers worked on appeals for John Wallace, from the very day of his
sentencing. He was a good client, never interfering, did not even seem to
make suggestions. He was leaving the court "doings" to A. L. Henson and
to Gus Huddleston and to the other lawyers.

The attorneys were very busy. On June 21, 1948, three days after Judge Boykin
announced his sentence, they appealed the electrocution date of July 30th. That appeal was turned down nearly two months later. Wallace had now escaped his first
electrocution date. Henson then appealed on November 17th to the Georgia Supreme
Court asking for a new trial. On New Years Day, the Georgia Supreme Court upheld
the Coweta County jury's verdict. Relentlessly, the appeals were made and denied.
His announced execution date, May 6, 1949, was postponed.

During that time, John Wallace sat in his cell, smoking cigarettes and writing
letters when he did not have visitors. Sheriff Potts dropped in from time to time and
they talked like old friends which, according to J. C. Otwell, they were.

His friend Henry Mobley, who was now in prison in Atlanta, was a letter writer, too. But Mobley's letters exhibited great depression, while John was usually optimistic and truly believed that he would be saved from his death sentence.

John saved twenty-seven of Mobley's letters. Josephine wrote letters to John and he saved fifty of them. She also sent him poems—some plaintive and some funny and he saved them, too.

Being very creative, her poems ranged from funny verses to lyrical poems which spoke of flower gardens, of changing seasons, of moon, stars. "I hope this miniature lyric poem will fit in your billfold"

WHILE THE WORLD IS WAITING FOR A SONG

While the world is waiting for a song
And while it waits
I'll sing this song to you,
I love you truly,
Always, and forever.
Though we're apart now,
I'll leave you never.
The early dawn, midday, twilight
Or moon glow
At the thought of you,
My heart beats fast, then slow.
While the world is waiting for a song
And while it waits
I'll sing this song to you,
I love you
I love you
I love you truly.

She made four ties for him, using thin, iridescent fabric that she had earlier used to decorate a picture of herself which she sent to him. He would have never worn the ties but he kept them and later gave them to Dorothy to keep. She did.

Other friends and family members wrote to him while he was in the Newnan jail for a year and a half and in the Atlanta Tower for nine months and in Reidsville for eight days. He kept fourteen letters from Mr. and Mrs. Toni Lane; seven from Edgar Jones; eighteen from Mrs. Nora Edwards; nine from Helen Hammett; five from C. M. Hammond; Mrs. George Lewis wrote him three times; James Taylor, five times. In all, John Wallace saved 147 letters from forty-five different friends and family members.

May Turner, one of John's trusted farm workers, often wrote him of the crops and of the weather which was so important in the planting and harvesting of the vegetables, the cotton, and the corn. He must have been distraught that there was no news of his dairy farm but he knew that the magnificent Guernsey cows had all been sold at the auction of July 13, 1948. Nevertheless, John and May rejoiced at the large crop of nuts that were gathered the falls of 1948 and 1949. He even got her to send some pecans to some friends out in La Feria and Santa Rosa, Texas.

His aunt, Lura Wallace Harrell, wrote him frequently when she had time from her duties as a teacher in the West Point public schools where she taught for thirty-five years. A note in a Chambers County, Alabama publication states, "The effect of this beloved teacher on countless students is limitless." Her son, Roy Harrell, also wrote to him. Cousin Roy was supportive of John in countless ways.

The letters Wallace received were optimistic about his chances of coming home. The letters gave news about family illnesses and sometimes a death "back home" was reported. The letters often included Bible verses and prayers such as the ones he got from the minister and the congregation of the Chipley Methodist Church where his wife still attended.

John Wallace was busy writing letters. In one of his many letters, he wrote a friend who was living in Texas, "Know you will be quite busy with such a nice crop of carrots. I have quite a few visitors and folks here have eased up quite a bit . . . Mr. Smith, who works here, went to town with me on December 22nd and I 'X-mas' shopped a bit." As with most of his letters, he ended it with, "Give my love to your family."

He wrote to Dorothy most often. She was the baby who was born right before he went into the Army, who was now thirty years old. He also wrote Willie, her mother. Willie was about his age, she being born October 29, 1895 and he June 12, 1896. Willie was nearer the same age as Jean, his sister. These two, Willie and Jean, had continued their long friendship which began when the Wallaces, living in Alabama, visited in Meriwether County.

On a Sunday night, in jail, John wrote,

> *Dear Dottie,*
>
> *Who should come in yesterday about 3:00 pm but "Mrs. Wallace"? She said that she just decided to come see what had happened to me. Mr. Potts come down and let her in and she left at 7:00 on the train for Chipley.*
>
> *She plans to go to Columbus tomorrow to try and get employment. I don't know how she will come out. Says that she is to see Piggie Gates who works with a real-estate company and also going to contact Dr. Gancy.*
>
> *She had only $16–17 to her name. I told her the only thing I could do was send her down to Caps if she gets hungry. So just go see what she could find out and if it came to the worst, she could go down to Caps, the foreman, and do the cooking and let May go to the fields.*

(Wallace did not seem overly concerned about Josephine.)

> *This a.m. about 10:30, Otis, Aubrey Gene, Todd and Middlebrooks came by. They went on to see Henry. Mr. Roy Durham, Ashley and Dr. Lipps came and some men from the Valley came to the fence. They had been to see Henry.*
>
> *Mr. Durham said Henry was the worst dissatisfied person he had ever seen. He said that he actually believed that unless Henry changed his attitude that he would lose his mind.*

Now I'm sorry for Henry but if that is all the sense that he has the quickest he does it the better off he will be. He will at least be out of his misery. I can't see what he can expect so soon. I sure would be willing to stay longer than he has before I would expect to be set free. I would wonder what he would have done with a sentence such as I have hanging over me.

(John did not seem concerned about Henry, either.)

We got another party in my suite now. A man from LaGrange for white slavery, similar to a case that was up here at first. His wife came up at 6:00 and I got Mr. Potts to let her in to see him. He possibly will make bond in a day or two. He was overseas and I've traveled all over France, Germany, Belgium and England with him since yesterday a. m.

Heard from Aunt Lura in same mail Saturday.

Am enclosing a letter Josephine brought along and gave me. Just put it away for me. For what reason I don't know, but will like to keep it for awhile. Just wonder who the informant was. I told Josephine, though, that I thought the advice was good. However, I did not mean to take her life.

Wallace was referring to a letter that Josephine had received, telling her that John had told a visitor that he was eager to get out of jail for he "intended to kill her!" In the letter, Josephine also was told that it would be a good idea for her to stay away from Georgia and live in the Carolinas or West Virginia with some of her relatives who had moved away.

A move away would be good for Josephine, John Wallace agreed.

In a letter to Willie, John Wallace wrote:

I have heard nothing as yet. I called Sister Tuesday and she said she had planned to call Mr. Henson or did call him and found him out, so she too knew nothing. Since I feel so sure that I'll get another "kick-back," I'm not so interested to know what has been done, so long as things are at a status quo, I'm at least no worse off.

OUT OF IMMENSE CONCERN, Sister Jean wrote a letter to the newly elected governor, dated February 14, 1949:

The Honorable Herman E. Talmadge
Governor of Georgia
Atlanta, Georgia
Dear Governor Talmadge:

    It is with pride that I use this title to greet you. I almost said, "Dear Herman", since I remember you as that high school senior whom I once heard in a debate on the stage of the Druid Hills School. At that time I believed you would be an alumnus of whom we should be proud. You have not disappointed me.

    I never thought that into my life would come a tragedy such as the occasion for this letter. Knowing that you have received communications in regard to the conviction and death sentence of John Wallace, Meriwether County dairyman, I shall make this as brief as possible.

    John Wallace is my only brother. It is my belief that he is the victim of perjured testimony and a grossly mismanaged defense. Not realizing the seriousness of his situation at the beginning, he placed the matter in the hands of a country lawyer, Gus Huddleston, of Greenville, his friend and attorney for more than twenty years.

    After his family had cause to suspect animosity and crookedness on the part of certain Coweta County officers and feared that he would not receive a fair trial in that county, A. L. Henson was engaged as counsel. It was too late, however, for Mr. Henson to conduct the case as he would have done had he been put in charge of it at first. I believe he has done the best he could, but up to the present, his best has not been enough to save John from the electric chair.

    My brother took a man . . . and gave him a job, not knowing that he was an Army deserter with an assumed name. The man turned out to be a cattle thief. He was killed in Meriwether County by the accidental discharge of a shotgun while my brother was attempting to force from him information concerning the theft of a number of thoroughbred cows. This is the statement made by my brother when he was arrested by the Coweta County sheriff. I believe it to be the truth.

The Meriwether sheriff had gone to my brother's home the night before and told him the man would be released from jail in Greenville the next morning for lack of sufficient evidence. Unwisely, my brother pursued the man as he was leaving Greenville, overtook him at a tourist court near Moreland, forced him into a car and took him back to Meriwether County. The witnesses at the tourist camp testified that the man was killed there as my brother forced him into the car. The affidavits to the contrary were obtained too late for presentation at the trial.

I am not saying that my brother is innocent of wrong-doing, and in the light of legal developments, I cannot expect him to be set free, but I do know that he should not forfeit his life.

There is not a man in his community who had done more good for his fellow-man. When misfortune befell a neighbor, John Wallace was the first to be called. He never failed to respond to a request for aid of any kind. Having no children of his own, he helped financially with the education of three or more students at Young Harris College. He tenderly cared for his aged mother during a lingering illness from cancer. No mother ever had a kinder, more devoted son. A man like that cannot be a common criminal—a menace to society.

I know that under Georgia law, the Governor no longer has the authority to grant a pardon or to commute a death sentence, but the Board can do it. I have the highest respect for the personnel of the present Board, whom I know by reputation. I cannot believe that they will allow John Wallace to go to the electric chair, if they know the facts in the case.

Won't you use your influence where it can best help?

Hopefully yours,

Jean Wallace Mozley

Principal of Druid Hills Elementary School for twenty-two years.

Governor Talmadge replied that he had no authority but would turn her request over to the Board of Pardons and Paroles. If so, it was of no benefit, for again, in spite of the dramatic meeting, this appeal was swiftly turned down.

During the time that Wallace was back in the Newnan jail, he appeared to enjoy the visitors and the letters that he was continuing to get. He seemed to have believed there was some success being made in the constant appeals being made for new trials or at least the commutation of the death sentence to life imprisonment.

Jean wrote:

Dear Willie,

Just yesterday I had a letter from Pope saying that Cap and Gus had been back to see him and said Gus had to have $750. Pope went to see Roy Askew and was told that the bank couldn't lend any more money on collateral already held by the bank. Cap had all he could get and a crop failure.

I called Henson and arranged for him to go with Willis and me to see John this morning. We had an hour's visit with him in privacy. I told John and Henson that I wasn't going to send Gus Huddleston any more money. Henson said he didn't know what expenses Gus could have had in Newnan or here either. I gave Henson $750.00 for his expenses.

DURING THIS TIME, IN late 1949, some of John Wallace's friends were not so optimistic about his success in getting his death sentence commuted. They had become impatient and feared that he would not be saved.

Among themselves, they talked of forcing themselves into the loosely secure Newnan jail and getting him out. Then that plot was told around and some believed that a run on the jail was a possibility. The rumor came to Sheriff Lamar Potts. So, in late December, Potts had John Wallace moved from the Newnan jail to the Fulton County Jail in the Tower complex, the most secure prison in Georgia and said to be one of the four most formidable maximum security prisons in America.

He would stay in Atlanta until he was moved againto Reidsville.

13

Going to Atlanta

"There is really nothing here to write about. Tell ol' Dot that I still love her." — **John Wallace wrote from the Fulton Tower, January 19th, 1950**

Being moved from Newnan jail to the Fulton County Jail, a part of the Fulton Tower Complex, on McDonough Street in Atlanta must have been a traumatic experience for John Wallace. Unlike Newnan, where his visitors came and left at will, the Fulton Tower was rigidly controlled and well-organized.

Built in 1902, the Tower was not new to John Wallace for he had been in a similar prison before—in the late-twenties and again in the mid-thirties for bootlegging. This time, though, he was "in a holding position," that is, awaiting electrocution or being released. John Wallace probably knew that Al Capone, who had overseen the whiskey shipments from all over the United States during Prohibition days, had been sequestered in the Tower during 1932. John Wallace had even been to Chicago to see about his shipments. Perhaps he even had dealings with Al Capone there.

A Mr. Cromer was his warden and John Wallace said, "He was fair." However, Mr. Cromer would allow visitors only with his advance permission. "I was sorry that Otis didn't get in to see me," Wallace complained. "But he should have asked Henson to contact the prison when he knew he was coming."

Wallace sometimes angrily wrote Willie about his treatment in Coweta County. "When I think about that crowd down at Newnan . . . and how they ran over me and lied me into positions and situations that face me now, I get an empty feeling down in my stomach," he wrote in early January.

Also in his letter to Willie, "Had a letter from Henson today telling me that we would have a hearing here before the State Supreme Court which will be only a stepping stone to the U.S. Court. Seems to me that they could just give me the benefit of all my evidence as well as it could be done in Washington. This is going to cost a great deal of money and right now I don't know where it will be coming from." (His sister would provide it.)

THE TOWER WAS DIFFERENT in another way. There were more sophisticated programs for better mental and physical health. Each day the prisoners were given opportunities for planned programs of exercise both inside and outside their cells. They were often provided with religious speakers who gave devotionals and Bible study.

A few months after he was put in the Tower, Celestine Sibley, "the sweetheart of the print press," got permission to have an interview with him.

In her book, *Turned Funny*, she writes,

> *I went to see the fifty-eight-year old [he was only 54] prisoner a few months before he was electrocuted and found him affably directing the activities of the prisoners in his bull pen and optimistically predicting that he would not be electrocuted. He had gotten religion in jail, he said, and found scripture promising that he would be spared by prayer. Besides, he had Miss Mayhayley's word that he would live to be eighty-eight years old.*
>
> *"If there was a time when I hoped she was telling the truth, this is it," he told me.*

He told everyone he saw that he was at peace with his situation and believed that he would be going to Heaven when he died. In Heaven he would see those whom he had loved before, probably thinking of his mother. An Afterlife was his, he believed. Read Mathew 5: 21-22 and verse 38, he extolled.

After the experience with his new-found religion, his letters abruptly changed.

Until the end of his life, he expressed confidence that the Lord would lead him Home. But he expressed remorse only once, and that was the time he was in a LaGrange café talking to an employee.

14

Going to Tattnall Prison

"Mr. Potts came to Atlanta this a.m. and brought me down here. We arrived here a little past noon. I will grant that they were nice to me in the trip down here. We stopped in Jackson and I had a talk with Dr. H. T. Strickland ('Jappin')." — **John Wallace wrote, October 26, 1950**

John Wallace seemed surprised to see Lamar Potts when he woke up. Potts was standing by his bed in his cell. Following instructions, Wallace hastily gathered his things, his clothes, the letters and the poems he was keeping, the fruit that he had been given, his Bible that he read and had written some notes in, his cigarettes and his cigarette holder. He also had his gold watch with him still. Sheriff Potts helped him to get packed and ready to leave.

When Wallace got out of the Tower into the sunlight he saw three cars waiting to take him down to Reidsville. There were two state patrol cars and the Coweta County Sheriff's car. The cars were parked so that the sheriff's car would be riding between two state cars. Again, Potts was fearful that there were those who would try to "kidnap" him on the highway. He and the accompanying patrolmen were prepared for a planned attempt to rescue John Wallace somewhere along the road to Reidsville, some one hundred and seventy-five miles away.

When Wallace got into Sheriff Potts's car he saw that old friend Sergeant J. C. Otwell was the driver; Lamar Potts would sit beside Otwell. John would ride in the back seat, handcuffed to Pete Bedenbaugh. The three cars cautiously moved out of downtown Atlanta, with radio messages going back and forth between the three vehicles. Sheriff Potts later said that his early fears that that there would be an interception were soon forgotten.

John Wallace had been expecting to talk with his only nephew, Willis, Jean's son, who visited him often, especially now that he was in Atlanta where Willis lived and worked. Before leaving the Tower, he asked Mr. Cromer to explain his absence to Willis when he arrived that he unexpectedly had to leave and to ask him to come on down to Reidsville. And, he added, please let Mr. Henson and Mr. Pope Davis know that he had left the Tower. It appeared urgent that he talk with each of the men "about some business matters."

Wallace had already gotten out his Bible and written some notes:

> *I was convicted in Newnan, Ga. June 1948 for a crime I did not commit in Coweta County or any other place. And that is the truth. Every witness used by the Sheriff lied about me. The blood on my clothes was planted by persons unknown to me. Steve Smith and Mrs. Hannah lied. Mayhayley Lancaster lied and Mr. Lucus of the Federal Alcohol Unit lied.*
>
> *Turner was in good health when he left Coweta County April 20, 1948. That is the truth so help me God. Tom Strickland was present when Turner was accidentally killed near Durand, Ga.*
>
> *John Wallace*

ON ANOTHER EMPTY SPACE in his King James Version of *The Holy Bible*, containing the old and new testaments, he scribbled,

> *"Tom Strickland could have told the truth and possibly helped save my life."*

(The next week, when he was in Tattnall Prison in Reidsville, he would give his Bible to Dorothy Dunlap, to keep.)

ON THE WAY TO Reidsville, going down Highway 57, they would pass through Jackson, Georgia. Against the advice of Pete Bedenbaugh, there was a brief stop for John to have a talk with his cousin. Barnes, in her book, *Murder in Coweta County*, describes this visit with his dentist/cousin as an unpleasant meeting. John Wallace did not remember it that way.

Then they were on their way again.

When they arrived at Tattnall Prison, John was assigned a room on death row. He profusely thanked Sergeant Otwell and Sheriff Potts for his pleasant day, but added, "Lamar, you know you are wasting your time coming all this way when I'll be out soon."

With Pete Bedenbaugh, with whom he had ridden shackled in the back seat, he became "huffed up" when Pete asked if he could have his hat, the one he was wearing. "Why would you want my hat?" he asked in a very loud voice. He then snatched it off and slung it at Pete, who treasured it for many years until it was burned up in a house fire.

Sheriff Potts quickly turned to Pete and reprimanded him for the request, realizing that Wallace was being told that he would no longer have use for a hat. John did not like Pete anyway and had told him on the way down, "You know, Pete, you are one of the ones I intend to kill when I get out of here!" Pete later said he only smiled at him, confident that he would not be getting out of Tattnall Prison in Reidsville, Georgia, to kill anyone. He also thought that Wallace maybe was just teasing him for they had known one another in both pleasant and unpleasant experiences for many years.

John asked Sheriff Potts again to get in touch with Mr. Askew and with Mr. Davis, for he desperately needed to talk with them. He also asked Potts to try to get Gus Huddleston to locate Jack Allen, the attorney for Tom Strickland, for he was still hoping that his cousin would come forth and admit that he had been with John and would describe the scene where Wallace had accidentally shot Turner. Sheriff Potts agreed to carry out his requests.

John wrote to Dorothy immediately after getting into his room:

> *I hardly know how to begin or what to say. Seems, dear little girl, that my days are really numbered now.*

He said that he wanted both Roy (Harrell or Askew) and Willis to know about all the plans he had made with Pope. He asked her to call Sister.

Robert Balkcom, the warden at Tattnall, came into his room and assured Wallace that it would be fine to have visitors. Warden Balkcom probably had no idea how many visitors would come during the next seven days. John Wallace had so many good friends who cared for him.

He also had business to take care of if he was really going to die—business like planning a funeral.

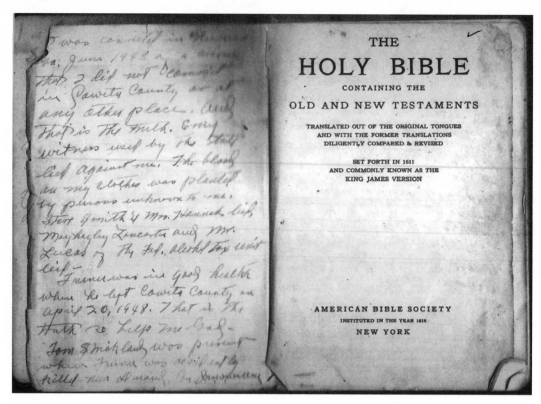

Pages from Wallace's Bible, in which he wrote during his final days.

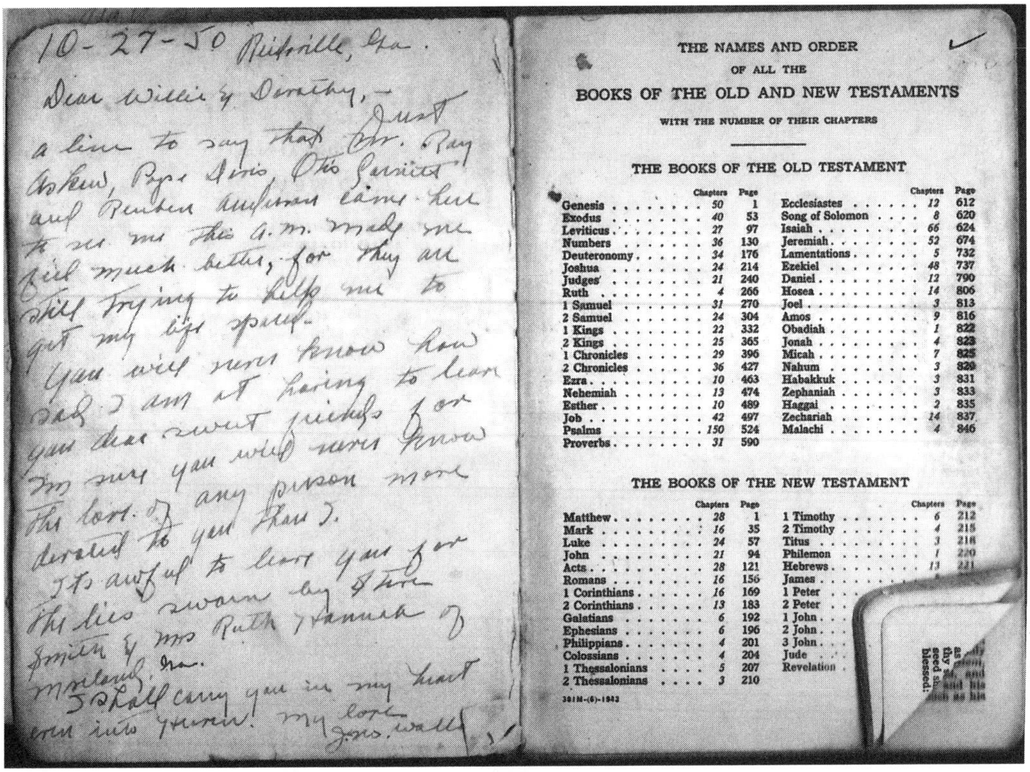

Handwritten letter (left page):

10-27-50 Reidsville, Ga.

Dear Willie & Dorothy, — Just a line to say that Dr. Ray Askew, Pope Davis, Otis Garrick and Reuben Dickerson came here to see me this a.m. made me feel much better, for they are still trying to help me to get my life spared.

You will never know how sad I am at having to leave you dear sweet friends for I'm sure you would never know the lost of any person more devoted to you than I.

It's awful to lose your for the lies sworn by Steve Smith & Mrs Ruth Hannah of Moreland, Ga.

I shall carry you in my heart even into yonder! My love, Jno. Wallace

Printed (right page):

THE NAMES AND ORDER

OF ALL THE

BOOKS OF THE OLD AND NEW TESTAMENTS

WITH THE NUMBER OF THEIR CHAPTERS

THE BOOKS OF THE OLD TESTAMENT

	Chapters	Page		Chapters	Page
Genesis	50	1	Ecclesiastes	12	612
Exodus	40	53	Song of Solomon	8	620
Leviticus	27	97	Isaiah	66	624
Numbers	36	130	Jeremiah	52	674
Deuteronomy	34	176	Lamentations	5	732
Joshua	24	214	Ezekiel	48	737
Judges	21	240	Daniel	12	790
Ruth	4	266	Hosea	14	806
1 Samuel	31	270	Joel	3	813
2 Samuel	24	304	Amos	9	816
1 Kings	22	332	Obadiah	1	822
2 Kings	25	365	Jonah	4	823
1 Chronicles	29	396	Micah	7	825
2 Chronicles	36	427	Nahum	3	829
Ezra	10	463	Habakkuk	3	831
Nehemiah	13	474	Zephaniah	3	833
Esther	10	489	Haggai	2	835
Job	42	497	Zechariah	14	837
Psalms	150	524	Malachi	4	846
Proverbs	31	590			

THE BOOKS OF THE NEW TESTAMENT

	Chapters	Page		Chapters	Page
Matthew	28	1	1 Timothy	6	212
Mark	16	35	2 Timothy	4	215
Luke	24	57	Titus	3	218
John	21	94	Philemon	1	220
Acts	28	121	Hebrews	13	221
Romans	16	156	James		
1 Corinthians	16	169	1 Peter		
2 Corinthians	13	183	2 Peter		
Galatians	6	192	1 John		
Ephesians	6	196	2 John		
Philippians	4	201	3 John		
Colossians	4	204	Jude		
1 Thessalonians	5	207	Revelation		
2 Thessalonians	3	210			

381M-(6)-1942

Pages from Wallace's Bible, in which he wrote during his final days.

10-27-50

My love to Mattie
Lane. She was so
sweet to write me
all during my stay
from home.

May God bless her
and keep her in good
health for many, many
years into the future.

With sincere affection

Jno. Wallace

10-27-50

A word of appreciation
to Joe H. Dunlap for
his long friendship
and may his health
improve and may he
be spared to live a long
life.

It's awful to leave you
all and have my life
taken by Coweta County
and its Sheriff Lamar Potts
for a crime that was
never committed at any
place.

Tom Strickland could have
told the truth and possibly helped
out my life — my love to you —

Jno. Wallace

MP39

Pages from Wallace's Bible, in which he wrote during his final days.

15

Gone

"I am fully prepared for my final journey and God is walking with me and no evil will come my way." **— John Wallace wrote to Willie, near the end**

His days in the Tattnall Prison were not at all like the eight months he had spent in the Atlanta Tower. His getting "religion" while in Atlanta now gave him the peace which he may have always sought. He now sincerely believed in an Afterlife, where he would be reunited with those he loved.

The warden and the guards found time to visit with him that afternoon. The usual prisoners were often sad, morose, pessimistic and fearful of their eventual outcome. John Wallace was different. He had a great smile, hearty laugh, firm handshake and excellent manners.

Once he was settled into his room, the prison chaplain came to see him and together they prayed.

On Thursday, the 28th October, Pope brought Josephine to see him. John told her to write a letter to the Georgia Pardons and Paroles Board chairman, Mr. Edwin Everette. She did as she was told.

"Please reconsider and extend his time. I know he is innocent. Smilingly, Josephine Leath Wallace (Worldeye)."

JOSEPHINE HAD BEGUN TO add "worldeye" to her poems and letters, referring to the fantasy place where children and small animals happily lived together. But *"Smilingly?"*

His room was soon crowded with visitors who had long wanted to visit with him. Some of his former classmates from Young Harris College came to see him. Cousin Roy Harrell was there from West Point, Georgia. Holmes Clements and Harvey Anderson came to see him and reminisced about the time that they, their wives and Dorothy and Willie had gone, in two cars, with John and Josephine to Texas and then hired a tour guide to show them around in Juarez, Mexico. What a good time they all had!

The following day, Friday the 29th, Pope Davis was back and John Wallace dictated a will to him—a will which has never been found, nor probated. He signed a prepared deed of eighty-seven acres of prime timber and pasture lands to be given to the Chipley Boy Scouts, but in the name of the Chamber of Commerce, a device that may or may not have been legal.

The staff of the prison was probably awed by a visit from the Reverend Charles Allen on Saturday, the 29th. Reverend Allen was minister of Grace Methodist Church, the largest Methodist church in Georgia. Reverend Allen was well known for his columns in the Atlanta newspapers.

They probably did not know that Reverend Charles Allen's father, Reverend James Allen, had once been the minister of the Chipley Methodist Church. There, John had known the Allen family well and it was he who had met them at the train station when they first came to live there. He had seen that their personal possessions were delivered to the church parsonage, and the Allen family had never forgotten the many courtesies that John Wallace bestowed during the next twenty years. When Reverend Allen left the prison, John Wallace called out, "Charlie Allen just came to see me and has agreed to preach my funeral!" Ten years later, Charles

Allen would go to the First Methodist Church in Houston, Texas, which, under his leadership, became the largest Methodist church in the world!

On Sunday afternoon, October 31st, Pope Davis was back with Roy Askew, his local banker from Chipley. When they were talking about land dealings, Mr. Askew pointed out that John was not leaving anything to Josephine. Wallace replied, "Let her get a job."

On Monday, November 1st, Hugh Park of the *Atlanta Journal* newspaper interviewed Wallace. While slowly dragging on a cigarette and speaking in a matter-of-fact voice with no show of tremor or any other emotion, Wallace told Park, "I am innocent of William Turner's murder. It was an accident. I never laid my hands on him to kill him. My gun went off. I am waiting to meet Turner face to face any time in the hereafter." Wallace also told Park that God had spoken to him and said, "He will guide me to His home safely." After a long pause, Wallace then said, "I fear no man and have never feared any man or foe."

Wallace then turned to those who were standing around the famous reporter, and said, "I want you gentlemen to pray that my soul will find a permanent resting place."

On Tuesday, November 2nd, Allen Lumpkin Henson drove down from his Atlanta law office to tell him the bad news: "We have done all that we could. We have no new procedure in mind. We still stand by and diligently look out for something which will commend itself to the courts, and we will make the best use of it if possible." It was now over. Over.

Wallace could have seen Henson out of a prison window as he spoke to newspaper reporters who were standing outside the prison gates, waiting for any news. Henson reminded the representatives of the state media that he had taken appeals to the state and federal Supreme Courts and to the Georgia Pardons and Parole Board in a long, long series of legal maneuvers which had now completely exhausted Wallace's financial resources. When he finished his talk with the reporters, Henson shrugged his shoulders and walked away.

John Wallace found time to write more letters. Some were thank you letters such as the one he wrote to the O. C. Hardaway family who were among the friends who had supplied him with cigarettes and personal clothing items during the last two and a half years when he was incarcerated in Newnan, in Atlanta and now in Reidsville.

He also wrote to Willie:

Dear Willie,

This thing of dying by the hour is a terrible process which I trust that those who I love never experience. The only consolation that can be gained is that I know when I leave this world and where I am going. That could be classified as a privilege.

I appreciate Jean's efforts and prayers and am confident that she is a most devout Christian.

I'm happy that you and Dorothy can cherish the memories of the most pleasant hours spent together and assure you that I shall carry the very same thoughts along and to and through the last moments of life.

I am fully prepared for my final journey and God is walking with me and no evil will come my way.

I shall rejoice when you all shall unite with me in a Land filled with love.

May you and Dot pray that my soul shall rest in Glory.

Good-bye and I'll see you in my dreams.

John

Jean and son, Willis, came to see him. Jim, her husband had died five months before, in June of 1950.

When she got home, she wrote her friend, Willie:

Henson's secretary said that there is nothing to be done for John to delay the electrocution.

I talked to Pope today and he said he would see you and all arrangements would be made according to John's plans. I asked him to put the funeral at three, instead of two, for that would be a more convenient time. I will see you Saturday if nothing is done to change our plans, and I am much afraid that there won't be any change.

You and Pope talk over the pall-bearers. I haven't talked with anybody but Roy Askew and I will ask Cousin Roy Harrell. So you and Pope get six or four more.

Love,

Jean

John Wallace continued to make his funeral and burial plans. He wrote this to Dorothy:

Jean and Willis came today and said they would come by your house and talk with you both about my plans. I have decided that I want to be buried as near to you as possible, even though it calls for me to be buried in the Chipley Cemetery. I'll be nearer so you all can know how my heart is filled with love for you both. Let me lie next to Joe, Jr. and then you, Dorothy, and Willie and Joe come in rotation. Let me be next to those who I love best if that can be worked out satisfactorily.

The one thing I can leave with you is a heart filled with love for I'm sure you never have, nor will ever, have a more devoted love than mine.

Then take hold of me for now is near the "Hour to say good-bye"

May we all get together in Heaven.

I'm now, so, so sad.

John

WHEN JOSEPHINE CAME AGAIN he told her that all the plans for his funeral had already been made by Pope and his sister. He said that Josephine was satisfied and went away.

His chosen undertaker, V. H. Hooks, came from Metter, Georgia, fifty miles away where Wallace had insisted he be taken if the electrocution took place, to which he was increasingly resigned. He told the undertaker that, should he die, he wanted to be promptly taken to his mortuary in Metter. He also told him that he wanted to be buried in his new, never-worn blue silk pajamas.

While the days were filled with old friends and former attorneys, John Wallace eagerly waited for Dorothy and Willie Dunlap to come to see him. When they got there he gave them his watch, his cigarette holder, all of the letters that he had with him and his personal Bible with messages written inside.

THREE MINISTERS FROM THE Hamilton and Chipley Baptist churches came to pray with him. He said he regretted that the minister of the Chipley Methodist did not come and hoped that did not mean that he could not be buried from his church. He knew he was not a member.

That evening, he wrote:

Dear Dot,

Your sweet letter came today and it was a joy to read the kind things therein.

You will never know how I'm being torn apart over the fact that death is only a short time now before it comes to carry me where I'll never have your love and affection in my life.

My memories carry me back to the many times that we spent joyously together, all the places we went and how happy were the hours we shared together.

The fact of having your love even until "death doeth us part" will help take the pangs out of death.

Stay the sweet, pure, good, devoted and loyal little girl you have always been to me and then when God calls you from this life, you will find me waiting to embrace you when we meet in Heaven. Nobody has or will in the future mean what we have for each other.

Be strong and brave and keep Satan behind you. He will try to destroy your soul but God will carry you safely through—only trust Him, only trust Him. Remember now that I want to rest by your side so see that the proper space is provided.

Come by Chipley on some Sunday afternoon and sit near me and pray that I may feel your presence.

Now, darling little girl, I'll now say goodbye for possibly and probably my last

good-bye to you while I live. I'll be singing love songs in my heart when I draw my
last breath of life.

Be sweet, my sweet. I'll be waiting. I'll see you in my dreams.
John
My watch and pen are yours as promised.

(More than fifty years later, Dorothy pointed out his watch to one of her neighbors. When the neighbor picked it up to look at it more closely, the watch began to loudly "click,click,click . . . .")

Later that day he wrote Louise, the wife of Henry Mobley (who was still in a Georgia prison).

Dear Louise,

You are aware that under the present schedule I now have only a few hours left on this earth. I have given Mr. Roy Askew a statement that will explain for those who may be interested the true facts that make up the case for Henry, Herring and Tom who are now so unjustly being denied their freedom.

I will leave a letter for Henry, Friday morning, should I go on a journey to a far and distant land. Now, Louise, I fear no evil for my Savior is now holding my hand and leading me to the Place that He went to prepare for those who love the Lord.

You will find enclosed herewith a dollar which I have invested for you when I received it on Xmas, 1949. After I have gone, you take it to Mr. Roy Askew and give it to him to invest. It takes time for a tree to grow.

May God ever bless you Louise, and protect you from all harm.

With a heart filled with love from one friend to another.

Jno. Wallace,
Mr. John to you, in your way.

THAT NIGHT, WALLACE REFUSED any special supper but lustily ate the common prison fare of chili, creamed potatoes, snap beans, cornbread, coffee, and egg custard. After another prayer with the prison chaplain, Wallace stretched out on his cot and slept soundly throughout the night.

In the morning, November 3rd, John Wallace was up early and still writing letters:

Dear Henry,

Now, Henry, with only a few hours left to live and while I'm in a good mind and in full control of my mental faculties, I want to write you a few facts that may be of interest to you as well as our friends.

Now Henry, you, Herring Sivell, and Tom Strickland know of your own knowledge that this is most untrue and that Turner was in good health at the time that Steve Smith and Mrs. Hannah claimed him to be dead. Herring was only with Turner a scant ten minutes and when his car developed a flat tire Turner and I got into your car with you and Tom. Turner entered your car unassisted and under his own power and without being forced even to get into your car. At no time did Herring ever attempt or try to do Turner any bodily harm and when Herring last saw Turner, Turner was not dead, neither did Turner have the appearance of having been done any injury that would produce death.

You and Tom Strickland had no part in the actual interception of Turner and had it been left to your efforts or acts, he, Turner, would never have been taken into custody on April 20, 1948. You and Tom Strickland were not present when Turner entered Sivell's car at Sunset Tourist Camp and it was after Turner, Sivell left Steve Smith's place at Moreland, Ga. that we, Sivell, Turner and I met you and Tom and at that time you turned your car around and followed us to the point that Sivell's car developed the flat tire.

Now at this time Turner, as above stated, was not dead, but very much alive and in good health.

Upon Turner and I entering your car we then proceeded into Meriwether County, you were driving the car, I sitting on your right and Strickland and Turner occupying the rear of your car.

Now, Henry, I trust that you be soon permitted to return to your family and in a weak way I have tried to leave behind a few bequests and in these you, Bob, and Louise have been included. May you remember me as your friend and accept my best wishes for a long and successful life and may when you depart from this earth be together in House that our Lord and Savior Jesus Christ has told us that He had gone to prepare for us.

I also at this time wish to clear up a few facts as to what Tom Strickland knows about and his connection with the circumstances which led up and included Tom, who was present when Turner lost his life.

I have to go now, Henry, and may God bless you and may we meet in Heaven.

Sincerely,

John Wallace.

Wallace did not tell Henry of the bequest of four hundred acres of land.

TWO HOURS BEFORE THE scheduled electrocution, Wallace was continuing to insist that he was innocent.

Again he spoke to reporter Park, "I had intended to send his body to his folks. But they put me into jail before I could attend to that."

He added, "I view my future just like I view you. I fear no man and have never feared any man or anyone. I fear no evil. I've never been afraid of anything all my life. Last night I slept well for God spoke to me. He will guide me safely to his House where he has gone to prepare a place for me. I am on my way now."

John Wallace was finally speaking of Turner's body, something that he had never done before, saying that he did not burn William Turner's body, implying that someone else did or that his major body parts were buried.

Otis Cornett and Aubrey Smith of Chipley and Talmadge Gates of Hamilton stood by the reporter. "If he thinks of anything, we'll be there until the switch is pulled," Mr. Cornett said, and then added, "He is what I call a Number One Man!"

Wallace joked with his friends and solemnly said to Cornett, who had been going every year to Wallace's Texas farm with him, "I don't believe we are going to make that trip to Texas together this summer. I'm going on ahead—you'll have to follow me."

At this point, Warden Robert P. Balkcom Jr. walked up to the jovial men and solemnly told Wallace that there was no indication of a reprieve. Wallace replied, "I've still got my hopes. The good Lord will take care of me."

Escorted by Warden Balkcom, Deputy Warden W. T. Wallace, and the Reverend W. L. Huggins, the prison chaplain, John Wallace left his cell at 10:35 and walked down the hall with them where they turned into the room where nearly forty men waited.

As Wallace reached the electric chair, he turned to the warden, and asked, "May I pray?"

Without an answer he turned to the foot of the massive white chair as if it were an altar, put his head close to the death-seat, and said, in a firm, strong voice, "Oh, God, I come before You and pray that You stand ready to receive me in Your House. I want to pray for my old uncle [Mozart] now past eighty years old, who will soon be coming to your home. I pray that we meet again in your Home. I pray for the Governor and the Pardons and Paroles Board who didn't know the facts."

Then with no tremor in his voice at all, his voice rose with emotion when he ended his prayer, "And, oh, God, I want to say before You, I am not guilty of this crime for which I am now paying the penalty."

He then rose to his feet and turned and smiled at some of the forty witnesses—old friends, prison staff, Pete Bedenbaugh, and several reporters. No family members of Wallace's or Turner's were present.

Wallace sat down on the hard seat of the electric chair.

The state electrician, who was paid seventy dollars for each electrocution, walked over and without a word, began strapping the electrodes on Wallace's right leg. The cuffs of Wallace's gray cotton pants were rolled up almost to his knees. His face looked pale and thin for a man who gave the impression of limitless strength. His prison shirt was unbuttoned at the collar and one could see a small paunch.

Wallace sat straight up in the chair and looked at the chaplain in front of him.

"Brother Huggins, do you think I've said everything I ought to say?"

"Yes, John," replied the chaplain, who had sat and prayed with him for many hours during the eight days he had been at Reidsville.

Then the electrician hurried into the main room coming from the embalming room, seven feet from the chair. The electrician had in his outstretched hands the death helmet with several wet sponges inside which were saturated with a saline solution which would better conduct the electricity.

"Do you want me to hold your hand?" asked the chaplain in a low voice.

"Please."

While a light towel-like mask was placed on John's face, the chaplain prayed the 23rd Psalm, and at the end of his prayer, he gently pulled away his hand. Wallace sat there in the stillness for a moment.

The group in the room was tensed in expectancy of the hum of the current when the three switches were thrown: one by Warden Wallace, another by a prison guard, and the third by the prison electrician. Instead, Wallace's voice came from behind the mask. Steady as though he were a little tired and was again saying farewell to his friends, the astonished persons heard him say, "Good-bye, men, I love everybody. I know I'm on my way to Heaven."

There was a hum heard in the room and Wallace snapped erect against the belt which was now across his lower chest. His hands, which had been lying loosely on the arms of the chair, turned a dark red and began to close. The chaplain walked across the room and stood at the door and wept.

The electric shock lasted for a minute. Drs. J. C. Collins and J. M. Hughes pronounced him dead at 10:49 only fourteen minutes after Wallace had strongly, proudly, calmly begun his death walk.

Federal Security Agency
U. S. Public Health Service

GEORGIA DEPARTMENT OF PUBLIC HEALTH
CERTIFICATE OF DEATH 3

State File No. **25801**

BIRTH NO.   Militia Dist. No.   Custodian's No.

1. Place of Death		2. Usual Residence (Where deceased lived, II institutions residence before admission)	
(a) County **Tattnall**	**1645**	(a) State **Georgia** (b) County **Cowata**	
(b) City or Town **Reidsville**	(c) LENGTH OF STAY (In this place) **9 Days**	(c) City or Town **Newnan**	LENGTH OF STAY (In this place)
(II Outside City or Town Limits, Add Rural)		(II Outside City or Town Limits, Add Rural)	
Name of Hosp. (d) or Institution **Georgia State Prison**		(d) Street Address or R. F. D. and Box No.	

3. NAME OF DECEASED (Type or Print)	a.(First) **JOHN**	b. (Middle) **NMI**	c. (Last) **WALLACE**	4. DATE OF DEATH	(Month) **11**	(Day) **3**	(Year) **50**

5. SEX **Male**	6. RACE **White**	7. MARRIED, NEVER MARRIED WIDOWED, DIVORCED (Specify) **Married**	8. II Married or Widowed Give Name of Spouse **Josphine Leath Wallace**	9. AGE (In years last birthday) **54**	IF UNDER 1 YEAR Months Days	IF UNDER 24 HRS. Hours Min.

10a. USUAL OCCUPATION (Give kind of work done during most of working life, even if retired) **Farmer**	10b. KIND OF BUSINESS OR INDUSTRY **NONE**	11. BIRTHPLACE (State or foreign country) **Chambers County, Ala.**	12. CITIZEN OF WHAT COUNTRY? **American**

13. FATHER'S NAME **DECEASED**	14. MOTHER'S MAIDEN NAME **DECEASED**

15. WAS DECEASED EVER IN U. S. ARMED FORCES? (Yes, no, or unknown)(II yes, give war or dates of service) **YES** **WORLD WAR #1**	16. SOCIAL SECURITY NO. **NONE**	17. INFORMANT **C E Buckner**

18. CAUSE OF DEATH Enter only one cause per line for (a), (b), and (c)	MEDICAL CERTIFICATION		INTERVAL BETWEEN ONSET AND DEATH
*See Reverse Side	I. Condition or complication (a) directly leading to Death* **LEGAL ELECTROCUTION**		
	Morbid condition, if any, giving (b) rise to above cause		
	(c) Underlying cause of death		
	II. OTHER SIGNIFICANT CONDITIONS Conditions contributing to the death but not related to the disease or condition causing death		

19a. DATE OF OPERATION	19b. MAJOR FINDINGS OF OPERATION	20. AUTOPSY? YES ☐ NO ☐

Diagnosis :	**985X**	**48**	2.	3.	4.	5.	6.	7.
Clinical ☐ Lab. ☐ X-Ray ☐								

21a. ACCIDENT SUICIDE HOMICIDE	(Specify)	21b. PLACE OF INJURY (e.g. in or about home, farm, factory, street, office bldg., etc.)	21c. (CITY OR TOWN)	(COUNTY)	(STATE)

21d. TIME OF INJURY	(Month)	(Day)	(Year)	(Hour) m.	21e. INJURY OCCURRED While at Work ☐ Not While at Work ☐	21f. HOW DID INJURY OCCUR?

22. I hereby certify that I attended the deceased from _____ , 19__ , to _____ , 19__ , that I last saw the deceased alive on **NOVEMBER 3RD** , 19 **50** , and that death occurred at **10:52a.** , from the causes and on the date stated above.

23a. SIGNATURE **J. M. (Hughes) M.D.** **L.C. COLLINS M.D.**	23b. ADDRESS **GLENNVILLE, GA.** **COLLINS , GA.**	23c. DATE SIGNED **11-3-50**

24a. BURIAL, CREMATION, REMOVAL (Specify) **Burial**	24b. DATE **11/4/50**	24c. NAME OF CEMETERY OR CREMATORY **Chipley Cemetery**	24d. LOCATION (City or Town) (County) (State) **Harris Co. Chipley, Ga.**

DATE REC'D BY LOCAL REG. **11-3-50**	REGISTRAR'S SIGNATURE **D M Lacy**	25. FUNERAL DIRECTOR **Hooks Mortuary** ADDRESS **Metter, Ga.**

REGISTRAR : CHECK CERTIFICATE CAREFULLY

Rev. 1-1-48   V. S. - 12

RECORD OF FUNERAL

Total No....45......... Yearly No...45......... Date of Entry...Nov. 4.........1950

Name of Deceased....John....Wallace.........White

☐ Married ☐ Single ☐ Widowed ☐ Divorced   (What Race)

Residence: Chipley Ga. R.F.D.   ☐ Husband ☐ Wife ☐ Widow   White
or..............of ⎰ Age of Husband or Wife (if living)   Years

Charge to Mr. Otis Cornett + J.P. Davis

Field	Complete Funeral (except outlays)........$	
Address. Chipley Ga.	Casket....................	298.00
Order given by Otis Cornett + Pope Davis	Burial Vault or Box............	
(or informant)	(State Kind)	
How Secured........	Embalming Body...........	
	(Name of Embalmer)	
If Veteran, State War........	Barber, $..........Hair Dressing, $........	
Occupation........	Dressing Body, $........Underwear, $........	
(Social Security Number)	Suit or Dress............	
Employer and Address........	(State Kind and Color)	
Date of Death 11-3-50 Friday	Slippers, $............Hose, $........	
(Date) (Hour)	Folding Chairs, $......Tarpaulin, $........	
Date of Birth........	Candelabrum, $........Candles, $........	
Age........54	Door Spray, $........Gloves, $........	
(Years) (Months) (Days)	Funeral Car, $........Ambulance, $........	
Date of Funeral 11-4-50 Sat. 3 P.M.	Limousines to Cemetery....@ $.	
(Date) (Day of Week) (Hour)	Extra Limousines..........@ $.	
Services at Chipley M.E. Church	Autos to R. R. Station......@ $.	
Clergyman Rev. Charles Allen	Getting Remains from Metter, Ga. 35 mi.	75.50
(Address)	Taking Remains to........	
Religion of the Deceased M.E.	Trip to Coroner's Inquest........	
Birthplace Chambers County Ala.	Delivering Box to........	
Resided in the State Tattnall	Deliver Flowers to........	
(or U.S. or City or County)(Years)(Months)	Removal Charges........	
Place of Death Tattnall State Prison	Procuring Burial Permit........	
Cause of Death Legal Electrocution	____Certif.Copies of Death Certificates No..	
	(State Physician's or Coroner's	
Contributory Causes........	Pall Bearer Service, $........Use of Chapel, $.	
Dr. J. M. Hughes - Glennville, Ga.	Gross Total for Sales Tax........$	
Certifying Physician Dr. J.C. Collins	Outlay for Lot........	
(Coroner)	Cremation........	
His Address Collins Ga.	Flowers, $....Palms, $....Matting, $........	
Name of Father........	Rental of Tent, $....of Temporary Vault, $.	
His Birthplace........	Opening of Grave or Tomb........	
Maiden Name of Mother........	Lining Grave, $......Lowering Device, $.	
Her Birthplace........	Outlay for Shipping Charges........	
Motor ⎱ Remains to........	Clergyman, $....Singers, $....Organist, $.	
Ship ⎰	Railroad ⎱ Tickets, $........Aero- Service, $.	
Size of Casket 7/4 Birmingham	or Motor ⎰ plane	
(Color)(Number)	Telegr., Phone, Cable or Radio Charges.	
Manufactured by Atlanta Casket Co.	Cash Advanced........	
Cemetery ⎱	Out of town Undertaker's Charges........	35.00
Crematory ⎰........	Personal Service........	

Diagram of Lot or Vault		
Lot No........	....line Death Notices in....Papers....	
Grave No........	(Names of Newspapers)	
Section No........	Sales Tax........	
Block No........	Total Footing of Bill........$	406.50
Owner........	Less............$	
	Balance............$	
	Entered into Ledger, page....or below.	

Date		Amount Paid	Balance	Date			Amount Paid	Balance
11-6-50	To Above Balance J.P. Davis	406.50	-0-		To Balance Forward		$	
	By Payment	$			By Payment		$	
	" "	$			" "		$	
	" "	$			" "		$	
	" "	$			" "		$	
	" "	$			" "		$	

16

Going to Chipley

"I can't remember what I said, but I sure remember the funeral."
— *Dr. Charles Allen, telephone conversation, July 2002*

As soon as the doctors declared John Wallace dead he was quickly shifted onto a gurney which had been waiting in the hall behind the electrocution room. The gurney with his supine body was pushed down the hall and carefully lifted down steep steps to a waiting hearse which had its motor running. Riding on top of his body was a small sack which held his blue silk pajamas.

His body's move to Metter was unusual. The Reidsville prison ordinarily embalmed its victims in the facility, but Wallace, for some reason still unknown, had adamantly refused this procedure. He insisted that his body go to the town of Metter. Mr. Hooks, the funeral home operator, had agreed to this plan the day before. This move fueled the fires of rumors which exist even today: "He warn't electrocuted at Reidsville. He escaped and went to Texas." Sometimes, it is to Mexico.

Passing through the Reidsville prison gates, the hearse, bearing the body of John Walton Wallace, sped to the little town of Metter, Georgia, which still has a sign saying, "Everything is better in Metter." There the gurney was unloaded and swiftly moved into the funeral home.

What happened in the Metter funeral home is not known. Surely, the prison clothes were removed and replaced with his chosen pajamas. There are no records of his body's being embalmed. The Metter Funeral Home was later paid only thirty-five dollars for its service.

The Maddox Funeral Home hearse had already arrived from LaGrange and was waiting with an empty casket which had been ordered by Pope Davis. The body was placed in the casket and the LaGrange hearse left for the funeral home in LaGrange.

The casket arrived just in time for a previously announced visitation time. The closed casket was to be viewed by invitation only. One close family friend complained that he drove all the way from outside Chipley to the funeral home in LaGrange but was not admitted for he "had no ticket," which was a plainly lettered statement of admittance.

Hastily placed flowers rested on the closed casket. The pallbearers—Roy Askew, Roy Harrell, Holmes Clements, Otis Cornett, Harvey Anderson, and Pope Davis —stood silently behind the casket while the invited ones moved slowly in and out of the room.

An hour later the door to the viewing room was closed and the pallbearers left for their homes in Chipley, Greenville, and West Point, Georgia.

The next morning the pallbearers returned to the funeral home and watched as the closed casket was placed into the hearse for its ride to the Chipley Methodist Church, going through Greenville, the Meriwether county seat. The new sheriff of Meriwether County had sent a car to lead the small procession to Chipley. As the cortege passed down the highway, approaching cars and trucks respectfully moved to the side of the road and waited and watched as the sheriff's car with its flashing blue rotating light, the long black hearse, and the pallbearers' two cars with their driving lights turned on, swiftly moved down the highway.

As the funeral cars slowly passed through Greenville and circled the courthouse, grim-faced spectators stood on the streets and on the steps of the courthouse and watched. Some wept.

The cortege picked up speed and continued on to the Chipley church. The funeral was to begin at three.

On time, the hearse came close to the door of the church and the pallbearers moved the casket into the church, placing it in front of the altar rail. Sitting up front was his sister Jean and her family and some of her closest friends from Decatur. Dorothy, Willie, and Joe Dunlap sat up front among other neighbors and some relatives from Meriwether County and from Chambers County, Alabama. Josephine had not come.

The church was silent except for soft music being played by the church pianist. There were no songs for Jean had suggested there be none. To preach the funeral sermon, the Reverend Charles Allen had returned to the church which he had attended as a small boy when his father was the minister.

There is no record of what Reverend Allen said. In a phone conversation when he was nearly ninety years old, he said he did not recall his words but he surely remembered the funeral!

When he finished his remarks, he moved to the outside door of the the church. He resolutely walked into the dark, dismal day—the weather was not cooperating. The pallbearers had rolled the closed casket, following Reverend Allen, then carried it down the steep steps, moving silently among the large crowd of people who were standing outside the church. The small church had been filled since early afternoon, leaving only enough space up front for his sister and her family.

Once loaded, the hearse slowly moved a block away to the cemetery. A place for his casket waited beside the burial site of the Dunlap lot, at the edge of the cemetery on its north side, away from other family plots. Wallace's burial site was alone but closest to the grave of the young Dunlap boy, Joe Junior, who at age fourteen had been buried there more than twenty years earlier.

Again, another large group of people silently waited in the cemetery and watched when the hearse appeared and wound among the older graves to stop when it reached John Wallace's chosen site. The pallbearers carried the heavy casket and slid it onto the straps which were stretched over the waiting hole. Reverend Allen said a brief prayer and moved away. Sister Jean and her group followed him and went to their cars and rode away.

The funeral home director from LaGrange decided to let the casket of John Wallace rest until those who had waited so long could come near and pay their silent respects to the life of John Wallace. He later said that he expected to bury the casket in a short while, but, no, the people came and came.

It was nearly dark when the attendants moved forward and lowered the casket into the hard Georgia clay.

Above, interior of the church where Wallace's funeral was held. Right, Wallace's reputed pew in the church.

Above, Wallace grave. Left,
detail of his marker. Below,
Josephine's grave.

KEEP THE ETERNAL MEMORY
JUST REST IN PEACE
J E W

JOHN W. WALLACE
JUNE 12 1896
NOV 3 1950

JOSEPHINE ELIZTH
WALLACE
DEC 18 1912
JULY 2 2003

"TEIGE"

More cemetery views.

Dorothy Dunlap's home.

17

Afterwords

"He was the calmest man in the death chamber that I have ever seen in my eleven years of penal work." — **Warden Balkcom to a reporter, the day after the execution**

O n Monday, the 6th, after the funeral on Saturday, Pope Davis went to LaGrange and paid Maddox Funeral Home $406 with a personal check for the funeral and burial expenses of John Wallace.

Sometime after 1950, no one seems to know when, a small marker appeared, attached to the slab over the grave of John Wallace:

I Kept the Pleasant Memory. Just Rest in Peace. JLW

On November 5, 1954, a television show, *The Big Story*, was seen in the Atlanta area, about which A. L. Henson wrote:

Wallace was portrayed as a handsome, but sinister-looking man, six feet-two, never without a bullwhip in his hands. Cowering outside a richly appointed office were a haggard group of bedraggled tenant farmers, begging for bread. The televi-

sion program showed emaciated children, brow-beaten mothers, poorly dressed—all with starvation written upon their faces. Unbelievably, not a single representation bore the semblance of truth.

Henson was more appalled that Hugh Park, who had written the script, had received a $500 fee for "objective reporting."

After the execution in 1950, Henson resigned from the law firm of Harris, Henson, Spence and Gower, and became a judge in the Fulton County Civil Courts. He died at age sixty-eight, May 30, 1961.

Gus Huddleston continued with his law practice in Greenville until he died in 1953, three years after the death of John Wallace.

THE THREE ACCOMPLICES WERE paroled June 11, 1955 and received full pardons on January 15, 1962. In a request for an earlier parole, Herring Sivell wrote, "Frankly, I do not believe that if John Wallace had not returned and burned Wilson Turner's body after this was all over, that there would have been such rabid feelings among the people in that section of the state. It was impossible for us to get a fair and impartial trial based on the facts alone."

Albert Brooks lived a long and active life. In an interview with *Columbus Ledger-Enquirer* state editor Harry Franklin, when asked about John Wallace, Brooks quickly replied, "He was the nicest and finest man I ever knew." Brooks died in 1998 at the age of ninety-three where he had been living in the Starcrest Nursing Home in Newnan. He was survived by seven daughters and seven sons.

John's beloved Uncle Mozart Strickland died in 1952, leaving all his assets to his niece, Jean. Faithful Aunt Lura died in 1960; Pope Davis died July 8, 1962; Tom Strickland died in 1963; both Herring Sivell and helper Robert Lee Gates died in 1968; neighbor Joe Dunlap Sr., died in 1971, Sheriff Lamar Potts in 1971, bank president Roy Askew in 1979, Elzie Hancock in 1980, cousin Roy Harrell in 1986, Henry Mobley in 1988, and Albert Brooks outlived them all!

In 1976 Margaret Anne Barnes wrote the easy-to-read *Murder in Coweta*

County (earlier named "Malice, Aforethought"). In 1983 musician Johnny Cash bought the film rights to her book. In the CBS movie he portrayed Sheriff Lamar Potts, Andy Griffith was John Wallace, and June Carter Cash played Mayhayley Lancaster. Barnes died October 11, 2007. She left all her research materials to Emory University.

J. C. Otwell retired from the state highway patrol, worked at another job for awhile, and lived on in Madras, outside of Newnan, until he was eighty-five. He had used the grappling hook which was used by Wallace's helpers to pull the remains of William Turner from the well as a mailbox attachment. It, the cell where Wallace lived while in the Newnan jail, and one of the jurors' chairs are now in the warehouse of Crain's Oil and Gas Distributors in Newnan, Georgia.

Josephine worked for a small sock factory in Chipley for two years until it closed, then in a Pine Mountain restaurant, and once lived in Atlanta as a live-in helper. She built a small house on the edge of Pine Mountain when Pope Davis's estate was settled in 1962, for he had designated $7,894 to be paid to her in his will which he wrote in 1954. She was living in Chipley when, in February 1958, the voters of Chipley changed its name to Pine Mountain, now a flourishing tourist town, largely associated with popular Callaway Gardens. She later moved to the LaGrange area where she worked in a large department store and continued to write poetry. She died at age ninety-two and was quietly buried July 2, 2005. One of her poems would be a fitting epitaph:

WHEN DEATH COMES

> *When death come and*
> *Life shall be no more*
> *Our work is over and*
> *We have opened the last door*
> *Our thoughts are gone*
> *In what we call the far beyond*

We all hope
We leave behind
A pleasant memory
Of some kind.

On her marker with her name and the dates of her birth and death, there is found a significant Irish word, TEIGE, which means "poet." She was that.

The Boy Scouts got their acreage from the original Wallace lands and now enjoy its use, sometimes cutting timber for needed expenses. Henry Mobley also got 400 acres of land from John Wallace. Willie and Dorothy received three tracts of land, a 40-acre plat, a 113-acre plat and an additional plat of 241 acres, totaling 394 acres. The deeds were signed by Pope Davis on May 10, 1954.

As Miss Mayhayley Lancaster's house continued to disintegrate as her fame grew, given fresh publicity with the Wallace trial, her clientele grew. From the usual $1.10 for a prediction, she was now requiring $2.75. While defense attorneys made cracks about her presence as a witchdoctor, Solicitor Luther Wyatt put a stop to the subject, saying, "Call her a soothsayer, call her anything you like, but her testimony was never denied by anyone in the courtroom," according to an article in the *Atlanta Constitution*. Outside the courtroom, however, her testimony was denied.

John Wallace's lake filled again. A subdivision was developed around its clear, cool waters. The people who live on the formerly named Comer-Stovall Road, then Stovall Road, then called Strickland Road, were not surprised in 1996 when the road was officially named John Wallace Road. When tourists invaded the road, searching for his house, lake, and lands, someone removed "John" from the sign and it is now, just, Wallace Road. Most of the new residents have never heard of John Wallace.

Sister Jean retired as a respected and beloved school administrator. Her son, Willis, died in 1961, leaving a widow and three children. Many years later, when Jean was seventy-nine, she married a widowed Atlanta insurance company executive who was thought to be an heir to the Grant department stores, but after a year of marriage, he died. A year later, Jean married English-born printing magnate, John Harland, but he too lived only a short while. At age eighty-seven Jean died and was buried next to her first husband, James Willis Mozely, in the Decatur City Cemetery. She was a member of the Druid Hills United Methodist Church, the obituary said.

John Wallace's closest confidants, Willie, died in 1980, and Dorothy, in 2007.

When Dorothy died, at age eighty-nine, she had been living alone in the Dunlap home after the death of her parents. She carefully maintained John Wallace's personal possessions which included a picture of her and Josephine together, 147 letters to him from friends and relatives, Henry Mobley's 27 letters, 87 poems of Josephine's, four ties, a pearl-handled pistol, a gold watch, a fountain pen, a cigarette holder and his Bible.

MORE THAN A CENTURY has passed since John Walton Wallace was born in the two-story frame house in Glass, Alabama, and more than sixty years have passed since he ceased to live among us. The rumors are still spread of his not dying in the electric chair, in part because he insisted that his body be moved to Metter, Georgia, rather than being embalmed in the state prison in Reidsville. For the record, his body was not embalmed in Metter, either. No one ever saw the body after the stop in Metter. The casket was never opened.

Because of his detailed plans for his burial among those whom he loved most, I am convinced that he never thought of escaping from Reidsville. If there was a plan for him to escape, he would not have asked his beloved Dorothy to visit his grave. And of course there is the little matter of the forty witnesses who saw his electrocution. Yet the rumors persist.

Among his relatives, he was both respected and hated. A cousin's wife told the author, "I can't stand that man," yet her husband went around the area paying Wallace's bills long after November 3, 1950.

Many of his friends in Harris, Troup, and Meriwether counties remained loyal to his memory. To most of them, "He was a number one man!" However, many of the more affluent and well-connected persons in those counties deny his prominence and say he was not well-accepted in polite society.

I once had the opportunity to ask a member of Wallace's wife's family, "What did Josephine say about him?"

The young man replied, "She never mentioned his name in fifty years."

(Maybe we shouldn't have, either.)

Many questions about Wallace's life and death remain unanswered. However this account does serve a valuable purpose: it is a rebuttal of a book which covered the 1948 trial so very well yet left readers with incorrect information of Wallace's early life and failed to delve into the information that was available from state agencies, from additional witnesses, and from forensic science.

Acknowledgments

The research materials came from many sources gathered over the past six years. I am especially grateful to the staffs of the Georgia Board of Pardons and Paroles in Atlanta and the Alabama Department of Archives and History in Montgomery. The Coweta County Courthouse records in Newnan, Georgia; the Chipley/Pine Mountain Historical Society in Pine Mountain, Georgia; the Cobb Memorial Archives located in the H. Grady Bradshaw Library in Valley, Alabama; the Chambers County Courthouse in LaFayette, Alabama; the Troup County Archives in LaGrange, Georgia; and the Meriwether County Historical Society's archives in Greenville, Georgia were all very helpful.

Most useful was the collection of letters, poems, photographs, and personal items maintained by Miss Dorothy Dunlap for nearly sixty years lying around her house and closed up in a suitcase which had once belonged to John Wallace.

The technical skills and pure old know-how of dear friends Ron Williams, Jean Clark, Clark Johnson, Charlotte Kennedy, Dan Langford, David Dean, Winston Skinner, Carol Mozley, Earlene Strickland Scott, Carolyn Crawford Thorsen, Ken Askew, Pope Davis Jr., and Frank Davenport (current president of the Chipley/Pine Mountain Historical Society) were very helpful. Ms. Malinda Brooks was a valuable resource with her excellent genealogical skills! Mike Freeman, retired longtime staff member of the Georgia Board of Pardons and Paroles was very helpful in the earlier days of my research. Unnamed forensic medical personnel with the Alabama Department of Public Health shed light up on the technicalities of body decomposition and cremation processes. My son, Russell Moore, made all the difference as he kept my old computer in working order over the past few years.

Without these persons, the publisher, NewSouth Books, would have gotten a whole heap of problems with spelling, punctuation, grammar and sentence structure, plus, the book would have missed a lot of good, current information! I am so very grateful for their help.

The photographs came from Carl Summers, Herbert Bridges, Winston Skinner, Sally Mabon, and from Miss Dunlap's records. The cover is a modified version of Jake Wagnon's collage.

Chronology of John Wallace

1840S	Wallace and Barrow families come to Chambers County, Alabama.
1860S	Davis and Strickland families come to Meriwether County, Georgia.
SEPTEMBER 1863	Thomas Welsey Wallace, father of John Wallace, born in Glass, Alabama.
DECEMBER 1864	Myrtice Strickland, mother of John Wallace, born in Meriwether County, Georgia.
1893	Welsey Wallace and Myrtice Strickland marry in Meriwether County, Georgia and move to Glass, Alabama.
DECEMBER 1894	Jean Wallace, sister of John Wallace, born.
JUNE 12, 1896	John Wallace born. Named John Walton Wallace.
1902	John Wallace enters Bryson Academy, local private school.
JULY 23, 1907	Welsey Wallace, prominent county leader and member of Chambers County Commission dies and is buried in West Point, Georgia cemetery.
MAY 1910	Myrtice and children, Jean and John, live with Lanier family in Fairfax, Alabama.
DECEMBER 16, 1912	Josephine Leath born in Blountstown, Florida.
1912	Myrtice and children, Jean and John, move to her parents' home in Meriwether County, Georgia.
1913-14	John Wallace attends Gordon Military Institute in Barnesville, Georgia.
1914-1916	John Wallace attends Young Harris Institute in Young Harris, Georgia.
FEBRUARY 1918	Dorothy Dunlap is born in Strickland home in Meriwether County, Georgia.
SEPTEMBER 1918	John Wallace is drafted into U S Army and assigned to Alabama Polytechnic Institute (now Auburn University) for military training.

NOVEMBER 1918	John Wallace is moved to Maryland hospital suffering from Spanish Flu.
JUNE 1919	John Wallace dismissed from hospital and returns to Meriwether County, Georgia farm.
SEPTEMBER 26, 1926	John Wallace arrested for making illegal whiskey.
MARCH 3, 1928	John Wallace tried and convicted and serves almost two years in Fulton Tower, Atlanta Federal Penitentiary. Uncle Mozart Strickland and neighbor Joe Dunlap also serve time in federal penitentiaries for same conviction.
LATE 1930	Wallace paroled from prison and returns home. .
1931	Meets Josephine Leath in Chipley, Georgia.
DECEMBER 1931	John Wallace marries Josephine Leath in elaborate ceremony at Meriwether Springs Hotel.
1934	John Wallace tried and convicted of whiskey violations and serves thirteen months in Fulton Tower, Atlanta Federal Prison.
1936	John Wallace paroled; returns home to dairy business.
JUNE 1938	Expands dairy business to LaGrange, Georgia.
1939	Discontinues "Superior Dairy" in LaGrange, Georgia.
MARCH 20, 1941	Myrtice Strickland dies and is buried by her husband in West Point, Georgia.
JUNE 1945	William Turner becomes sharecropper on Wallace farm.
APRIL 20, 1948	William Turner is killed by John Wallace.
JUNE 14, 1948	Wallace murder trial begins in Coweta County Courthouse, Newnan, Georgia.
JUNE 17, 1948	Wallace testifies for seven hours in trial.
JUNE 18, 1948	Jury returns guilty verdict for murder of William Turner. He is sentenced to death in the Georgia electric chair for murder of Turner.
1948–50	Multiple appeals for new trials. All denied.
NOVEMBER 3, 1950	John Wallace dies in electric chair at Tattnall Prison.
NOVEMBER 4, 1959	John Wallace funeral at Chipley Methodist Church, with burial in the town cemetery.

Index